KU-549-604

Preparing Materials for Open, Distance and Flexible Learning

An Action Guide
for Teachers and Trainers

DEREK ROWNTREE

KOGAN PAGE
Published in association with the
Institute of Educational Technology, Open University

This book is dedicated to the thousands of colleagues who – in workshops and consultancies over the last 30-odd years – have helped me shape up my own ideas about how to develop learning materials, even while I have been helping them shape up theirs.

First published in 1994

Kogan Page Limited
120 Pentonville Road
London N1 9JN

© Derek Rowntree, 1994

British Library Cataloguing in Publication Data

A CIP record for this book is available from the British Library.

ISBN 0 7494 1159 7

Typeset by the author
Printed and bound in Great Britain by
Biddles Ltd, Guildford and King's Lynn

Preparing Materials for Open, Distance and Flexible Learning

Open and Distance Learning Series

Series Editor: Fred Lockwood

Contents

photo by Mike Levers

Before we begin . . .

I don't know about you, but when I settle down to spend several hours with a book I like to have some mental image of what the author looks like. With a novel, I nearly always get a photograph of the author. With a non-fiction book I often do. But with materials for open, distance or flexible learning I almost never do. This strikes me as odd—especially when such materials are trying to be welcoming and user-friendly. I find myself spoken to as "you" by people who call themselves "I" or "we"—all quite intimate—and yet I have no idea of what they look like. Very often, I'm not even told who they are or what experience they have in the field they are writing about. I believe we should be told (and shown). What do you think?

So, that's why my picture is on show. What else might you find relevant to know about me? Possibly the fact that I have been working with materials-based learning for more than 30 years. First with "programmed learning", then "resource-based learning" and then, since 1970, with open/distance learning in the Open University—and in a variety of subject areas including arts, education, health care and management education. In recent years—partly through my consultancies and workshops for outside organizations—I have mostly been concerned with materials-based approaches to vocational training and professional updating. As well as learning materials, I have written several books, some of which are described at the end of this one.

Derek Rowntree, November 1993

So you want to develop learning materials?

Open learning? Distance learning? Flexible learning? Which are you concerned with? Maybe some combination of the three. Or perhaps your form of learning goes under another name. No matter. I guess you are unlikely to have picked up this book unless the words in its title seem to touch on your concerns.

Why?

In particular, you will probably be concerned with finding, adapting, developing—somehow or other obtaining— learning materials. Open, distance and flexible learners usually depend a lot on learning materials. This may be because there aren't enough teachers or trainers to give them constant attention. It may be because they want to learn on their own—at a time, pace and place of their own choice. It may be because they are learning to take responsibility for their own learning.

In what form?

Materials may take many forms—books, worksheets, audio and video-tapes, CBT packages, multi-media, to name but a few. How are you to "prepare" them? Do you have to write your own? Or can you buy them "off the shelf"? What will it all cost—in time, money and effort? Just what is involved?

This book should help you find answers to these questions. As a result, you should be more competent in the objectives you'll find overleaf.

Objectives

As a result of working through this book, you should be better able to:

- Specify the kind of materials your learners will need.
- Track down materials that may be suitable.
- Evaluate such materials using appropriate criteria.
- Customize materials that are not quite suitable as they stand.
- Write new materials suited to the needs of your learners.
- Edit materials and prepare them for the production process.
- Evaluate and improve your own materials.

These objectives relate to Units TD43–47 in the NVQ/SVQ— *Training and Development (Flexible and Open Learning)*.

How to use this action guide

As you'll have seen, this book is called "an action guide". That is, it's not just for browsing in. Nor is it meant to fill you up with hints and tips for use at some time in the future.

Rather, it's meant to guide you in doing something—**here and now**. It's meant to help you prepare your own learning material—step by step—starting as soon as you're ready.

Is this for you?

I assume that you already have some learners in mind. You have a fair idea of what they might need to learn. You are sure that learning materials could or must play a part in helping them learn. And you have decided—or been commissioned by "clients"—to prepare those materials.

Does that describe you?

I hope so, because that's the person I've written this book for.

How the guide works

In this guide, I aim to take you through three **stages** in preparing materials:

Stage 1   Planning your materials

Stage 2   Preparing for writing

Stage 3   Writing and re-writing.

In each stage you'll have a number of **development tasks** to carry out. I'll outline each task, give you some ideas about how to tackle it, and help you evaluate and improve on what you have produced.

What sequence?

I suggest you work through the stages in the order shown in the route map opposite. Within Stages 1 and 2, however, most of the tasks can be tackled in any order you choose.

But please don't imagine that you will work for a while on one particular task, complete it, and then move on to the next with never a backward glance. That's not the way it works. You'll soon find that **you will constantly need to look back to earlier tasks and review your decisions in the light of your more recent thinking**.

The hollow arrows near the right of the map are there to remind you of this need for review.

Route map for materials preparation

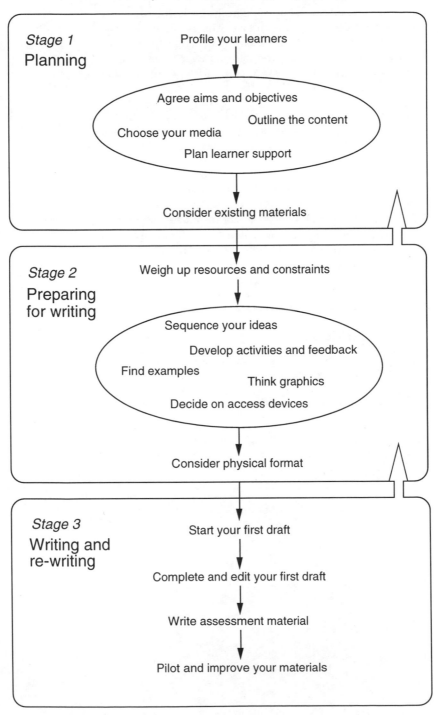

Stage 1
Planning

Profile your learners

Agree aims and objectives

Outline the content

Choose your media

Plan learner support

Consider existing materials

Stage 2
Preparing
for writing

Weigh up resources and constraints

Sequence your ideas

Develop activities and feedback

Find examples

Think graphics

Decide on access devices

Consider physical format

Stage 3
Writing and
re-writing

Start your first draft

Complete and edit your first draft

Write assessment material

Pilot and improve your materials

Getting information

I have been as sparing as possible in the background information I've given for each task. This is partly because you may have a lot of the necessary knowledge already. In that case, I'll be prompting you to bring your experience into play. And, if some of it is new to you, I'll be prompting you to find out more for yourself.

After a brief introduction to each task, I offer you a number of single page "displays"—usually contained within a frame. They contain checklists, examples, or hints and tips to help you with that task.

But these displays are suggestive rather than exhaustive. They do not pretend to tell you everything that new writers might need to know. Rather, they are meant to get you thinking and talking. They are usually very condensed and you may want to "unpack" some of them. Nearly every one of them could be used (and many have been), as the basis for a couple of hours of activity and discussion on one of my workshops. (You too may want to use them in that way.)

Other sources

"All right, but how am I to get information that's not in your book?" you may ask. There are two main sources:

- For each task, I suggest **further reading** you might do. (See the opposite page.)

- I also urge you to consult with **colleagues**—and with **learners** also if they are available.

Start your own reference library

The books I refer you to most often are ones I know especially well—because I wrote them. I refer to them, for short, as TTSI, EXPLODL, DCfS. These abbreviations stand for:

- *Teaching Through Self-instruction*, published by Kogan Page, London, 1990

- *Exploring Open and Distance Learning*, published by Kogan Page, London, 1992

- *Developing Courses for Students*, published by Paul Chapman, London, 1981

You may already have one or more of these books on your shelves. If not, you might like to consider laying them in as the basis of your professional library on open learning. I'll mention other useful titles as we go along. (And see the "Further reading" list at the back of the book.)

Collecting materials

I also suggest you start looking for interesting **open learning materials** to add to your reference library. Novelists usually take a keen professional interest in reading other people's novels. Advertising copywriters keep a critical eye on other agency's advertisements. Screen-writers watch movies. Similarly, developers of open learning material can learn a lot by analysing what other developers are doing.

If you can't buy it, then beg, borrow or swap material. This way you'll gather a rich and growing pile of stuff to prime your pumps and perhaps set you off in new directions.

Getting support from other people

But much of the knowledge you will need is **not** in books. It is to be found in your contacts with other people. There are two kinds of contact you will find essential while working through this book:

- **Colleagues**. You'll see that, for every task, I suggest you check out your ideas or your draft materials with colleagues. The feedback they give you will then help you refine those ideas. I suggest you start looking for such colleagues straight away. Let them know what sort of support you'll be needing, and when.

- **Learners**. With some tasks, I suggest you consult learners also. Even more importantly, you'll need the help of learners in piloting your materials (Task 3d). So, where can you find some learners like those you'll be writing your materials for? How can you persuade them to give you the help you'll need? Let them know how much time you'll need from them, and when.

Emotional support

This book focuses on the tasks of writing. I don't have space to go into the emotional aspects. Yet developing learning materials can make unexpected demands on one's ability to handle stress. There comes a time in practically any challenging project when most of us will begin to feel less than equal to the task, to wonder whether we can satisfy the demands being made upon us (not least by ourselves) and to despair of ever finishing it. Materials preparation can also be an isolating activity, even within a group.

However, other people—when they are not being the cause of some of this stress—may also help us overcome it. Once your writing is well under way, try to get into **networking**. Do you know anyone, in your organization or in others, with whom you can swap ideas? You may find (as I do) that keeping in touch with other writers elsewhere helps you be both more critical and more creative about your own work on materials development. It may also help you keep sane.

What sort of materials?

Open, distance and flexible learners may need any of a variety of learning materials. I've listed some of them on the next page.

Which of these do you think **your** learners might need?

In this book I shall mostly talk about printed materials. Print is used far more than any other medium in open learning. But you will need to go through exactly the same development tasks if you are preparing audio-visual or technology-based materials. The same principles apply.

What are open learning materials?

You may well ask. I would say that open learning materials are materials put together in such a way that users can learn from them satisfactorily with less help than usual from a teacher.

We often talk of such materials as a "package". A package may be a single workbook. It may be a videotape or audiotape with a study guide. It may be a computer disc or a CD or a practical kit together with back-up notes. Almost anything that stores information can be part of a package.

Packages don't have to use more than one medium, though they often do. They don't even need to contain more than one item. What they do have to contain is a teacher in a state of suspended animation. Once the learner opens the package, that teacher is instantly at their service, ready to help them learn.

Some types of learning material

Printed material

☐ Books already published for the general reader.

☐ Textbooks and manuals, already published, or else specially written.

☐ Specially written "wrap around" study guides to go with material already published.

☐ Specially written self-teaching texts — "tutorials-in-print" or "action guides".

☐ Worksheets for use along with audiotape or videotape material, practical work, etc.

☐ Case studies.

☐ Briefing notes for untutored group activities—e.g. discussions or role-plays.

☐ Self-tests, project guides, notes on assignment requirements, reading lists, etc.

☐ Maps, charts, photographs, posters, etc.

☐ Newspapers, journals and periodicals.

☐ Handwritten notes passing between learners and tutor.

Audio-visual and technology-based material

☐ Audio-cassettes/audio CDs/discs.

☐ Slides or filmstrip.

☐ Film or film loops.

☐ Video-cassettes.

☐ Computer-based training (CBT) packages.

☐ Interactive video packages.

☐ Multi-media (CD-based) packages.

☐ You may also be interested in materials that take the form of **real objects**—e.g. equipment, real objects, specimens for the learner's individual use, perhaps in kits for practical work.

What's the difference?

So how does an open learning package differ from the resources that teachers and trainers may use in ordinary classroom teaching? How does it differ from textbooks, reference manuals, videos, off-air recordings, and so on? After all, it is possible to learn from these items also. Indeed, such items might even be **included** in a package.

The chief difference is that a package will have been designed with a more specific purpose in mind. It will be aimed at specific learners, specific objectives, specific competences. If it consists of more than one item, each will have a specific and separate role to play.

Even if there is only one item (e.g. a workbook), support staff may be expected to help the learners in certain specified ways. If the developers include existing resources, like textbooks or videos, they will "customize" those materials by adding a study guide that helps learners relate them to their specific needs.

Tricks of the trade?

Package developers use a number of techniques to help the learner learn. These techniques can be seen most clearly in printed workbooks and study guides. But similar ideas also underpin the teaching in effective open learning videos and audio material and in technology-based teaching.

If you've examined any open learning materials, you may know of these techniques already. (Look, for instance, through the sample pages from workbooks on pages 18–38.)

I've listed what I think are the main "tricks of the trade" on the opposite page.

Special features of open learning materials

- Clearly stated objectives.
- Advice about how to study the material.
- User-friendly, "You and I" style of writing.
- Shortish, manageable chunks of learning.
- Fewer words than usual per page (or screen).
- Plenty of helpful examples.
- References to the learners' experience.
- Illustrations used where they are better than words.
- Headings to help learners find their way around.
- Links to other media where appropriate.
- Obvious awareness of different learners' needs.
- Exercises that get the learners to use the material.
- Space for learners to write down their own ideas.
- Feedback to help learners check their own progress.
- Suggestions about getting help from other people.
o *Others you've noticed? (What?)*

NOTE: In recent years, many "ordinary" textbooks have adopted some of these features—so they are no longer peculiar to open learning materials.

Three types of open learning materials

Most open learning materials are built around

information + action.

That is, they generally provide information and expect the learner to act upon it. They can do this in at least three different ways. I call them:

- *Tell-and-test*
- *Tutorial-in-print*
- *Reflective action guide*

You may have noticed others.

Tell-and-test

The most basic approach is to provide many pages of unbroken reading (or viewing or listening to a tape)— followed by a self-test with answers provided. This is what I call the tell-and-test approach. It seems to be based on the lecture + questions format; or maybe that of a textbook chapter with "comprehension" questions at the end.

The effectiveness of this approach depends on the quality of the telling and on the helpfulness of the testing. At its best it can be lively and stimulating. At its worst, a dreary wodge of bumf—little more than an information pack which learners are left to manage as best they can.

Sometimes, the information offered is so minimal that the material might be described as "Remind-and-test"—or perhaps "Practise-and-test".

Tutorial in print

The tutorial-in-print style is quite common among open learning workbooks and some computer packages. It is meant to be like having a good coach or tutor, working with you one-to-one. Unlike the tell-and-test, this kind of material does not present a monologue. Instead, as a tutor might, it asks the learner questions ("activities") every few minutes to check that they have understood the ideas being discussed and can comment on them or apply them. Immediate feedback is given so that learners can check their answers before going on. This approach arose out of branching programmed learning which tried to create a kind of "dialogue" with the learner.

The tutorial-in-print style is perhaps most appropriate when there is a "body of knowledge" to be mastered. Here the aim is to help the learner take on board a new way of looking at things. The frequent activities help ensure that learners are keeping up with the argument. These activities focus on ideas and usually involve writing something down or tapping computer keys. The writer is able to give quite specific feedback because he or she knows the kind of thing that learners will have written. The learning is assumed to happen while the learner is interacting with the package.

Reflective action guide

The reflective action guide assumes that the important learning will take place away from the package. The material is offered as a guide to action elsewhere—in real situations, perhaps with other people.

The aim is not primarily to help learners master an existing body of knowledge so much as to help them pursue a personal project—developing their individual insights, or practising towards some kind of practical competence. The aim may be partly to do with learning to **see** the world in new ways but it will also involve learning to **act upon it** in new ways.

Notice, however, that we are not talking here of an action guide like a recipe book or a checklist for programming your video recorder. We are talking of a **reflective** action guide—one that requires learners to think critically about the why and how of what they are doing—and evaluate the outcomes.

The reflective action guide may have fewer activities than a tutorial-in-print but they are likely to be more time-consuming. The reader may spend far more time on the activities than on reading the text.

Also, the activities are more likely to be related to the learner's own situation than to sample situations or case studies posed by the author. Similarly , they are less likely to involve answering questions about what the author has said in the package. On the contrary, they are likely to involve going out to do something away from the package—like the "development activities" in this book.

The learner may well be expected to interact with other people as part of an activity. The author cannot know enough about the learner's situation to provide specific feedback, so the learner must gather his or her own.

The reflective action guide may contain checklists and job aids. It may be intended for use "if and when" the user needs to carry out a particular task (e.g. analyse a balance sheet or carry out an appraisal interview)—a sort of "just in time" use. This contrasts with the "front loading" use intended for much tutorial-in-print material— where the learner is expected to imbibe a body of knowledge so that he or she can apply it at any time from then on.

The ultimate form of reflective action guide may be the "package" provided for learners doing an independent project, as in certain Open University courses. Here, a 20-page booklet may set up the learner for weeks of activity. It may contain guidance about how to choose a topic, sources of data, techniques of analysis, forms of reporting, the role of the tutor, and so on. But it may contain nothing of substance that has to be learned. The substance is all "out there", in the real world.

What approach
*—or **combination** of approaches*
—might you want to use? Why?

Sample pages from open learning materials

Materials play a vital role in open learning. Yet developers are usually so busy that they don't get time to look at any materials other than those being used in their own organization. Sometimes, they don't even get to see materials used in other **sections** of their organization.

This is a pity. I believe that we can learn a great deal about the design and use of materials by reflecting on how other people do it. It doesn't matter if their subjects and their learners are very different from ours. In fact, it may be helpful because it can concentrate our attention on **how** the materials are teaching rather than on **what**.

The next few pages give you just a glimpse of the materials I keep on my shelf for reference. I have already urged you to start building up your own collection of samples. I suspect that, like me, you'd find it a stimulating resource.

Studying the samples

You may well have no professional interest at all in any of the subjects dealt with in these sample pages. That shouldn't matter. Just ask yourself:

- "What is the author doing to help the reader learn?"

- "Which of the three approaches mentioned so far (if any) does she or he seem to be using?"

- "What might be the pros and cons of using such an approach in my subject and with my learners?"

NOTE: *All the samples are from workbooks, but some of these were for use with other media—audiotapes, videos, computers or practical work. The originals were all A4 in size, and some were printed in more than one colour.*

The contributors

The 21 sample pages that follow are from open learning materials produced by the organizations listed below and are reprinted here with their kind permission.

The second example is from Kathy. It describes an incident from an Academic area of her life.

❝ How did I get started?

I was in the sixth form at school and wanted to go on to do science 'A' levels. The teachers insisted that we all had to do a German 'O' level because this would be important in getting a job later on.

How did I learn?

It was all classroom based, repeating exercises from the text book. I hated the German teacher, he made me feel completely inadequate. I used to get very anxious before the class because I knew he would make me look stupid in front of everyone else. Half way through the year I realised I wasn't learning much from the classes so I borrowed a self study kit, with tapes and books, and passed the exam on that.

Where did I learn?

I learned very little in the classroom. I passed the exam on what I learned at home from the self-study kit.

Why did I learn?

The only purpose of the learning was to pass the wretched exam.

What did I learn?

I suppose I learned how to put up with a lot of aggravation, but to come through anyway. I also learned that you don't have to rely on teachers and courses to learn things. I've been fairly independent in my approach to learning since then. It also gave me a block about learning languages which I still have. ❞

You will now be reflecting on your own descriptions of learning incidents to draw some very general conclusions about the sort of approaches you take to learning tasks, and the sort of situations in which you tend to learn well.

ACTIVITY

First choose a positive learning incident, one from which you felt you learned a lot, and which you generally enjoyed completing. Sean's example illustrates a generally positive learning experience.

Read through the description of the learning incident you have chosen (from those described on Activity Sheet 4). In order to summarise what you have learned about yourself as a learner, draw up a list of statements beginning with the phrase 'I am the sort of person who learns well when ....'. Complete as many summary statements as you can and record these on Activity Sheet 5.

Here are four statements Sean was able to make, drawing on his description of the learning incident given earlier.

❝ *I am the sort of person who learns well when ...*

... *there is a clear purpose to the learning*

... *I am in control of when, where and how the learning takes place*

... *I can draw on a variety of sources – books from the library, conversations with others, newspapers and government reports*

... *I can work on my own, but in cooperation with others.* ❞

Now choose a negative learning incident, one which you did not enjoy and which had some negative outcomes for you. Kathy's example illustrates a generally negative learning experience.
Read through the description of the learning incident you have chosen. Now draw up a list of summary statements beginning with the phrase 'I am the sort of person who does *not* learn well when ....' and record these on Activity Sheet 5 in the Portfolio.

Activity 1 Your own house's face

The purpose of this activity is to begin a design analysis of your own house, starting from the outside (the 'face' your house presents to you and your neighbours) and, in later activities, working inwards to the plan and other details. (Estimated activity time: about ½–1 hour.)

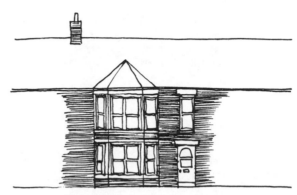

My drawing of the front of our house, from memory

1   From memory (i.e. do it straight away, without first going outside to look) draw the front of your house. Don't worry about details that you cannot remember, but try to make your drawing as clear and as detailed as you can, although obviously you probably won't be skilled at drawing and your attempt may in fact be fairly 'childish'. Try asking other members of your household to make their own drawings, too, without looking at each other's until you have all finished. (As with all these activities, my own attempt is shown alongside.)

2   Compare your drawings one with another. Are there any large differences between what you each remember and have drawn? Has someone in the family clearly got a better memory of all the details of the front of your house, or do you disagree among yourselves as to the details and their relative locations?

My daughter's drawing of the front of our house, from memory

3   Now go and look at the front of your house and compare the reality with the drawings. Are there any large differences between the reality and what is supposed to be represented on the drawings? Did you have a good visual memory of the front of your house, or have you not really looked carefully at it before? Try making another drawing from observation, to improve on your first attempt.

A photograph of my house (the one in the middle)

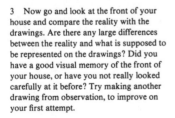

Retailing Basics

Hazard warning signs

Some products require special care when being handled or stored. Hazard warning signs appear on products to tell you what the hazards are.

If you have to use a product which is hazardous or if you may be exposed to one when cleaning up spillage, for example, remember to read the health and safety instructions which should appear on the packaging. This will enable you to deal with it safely.

It may be, for instance, that you should wear gloves or protective goggles.

 Go round the store looking for as many hazard signs as you can find.

Using the space below, draw four symbols which you have found and indicate what they mean.

1

2

3

4

8   TOLSTOY'S MORAL NEUTRALITY

8.1   'I have found', Tolstoy once said to a friend, 'that a story leaves a deeper impression when it is impossible to tell which side the author is on'. (See p. 45 for the full quotation.) As Tolstoy puts it, this might sound no more than a clever author's device; but I would suggest that it means something deeper.

8.2   Consider the question of 'taking sides' in a novel for a moment. It is surely very important in almost all the novels you have studied in this Course. (You will remember Graham Holderness's remarks about it in connection with *Wuthering Heights*; see Units 4–5). You can put it to yourself in this way: do the authors, at certain points in their novel, depend on your feeling *indignant*, or *gladdened*? Well, clearly, Jane Austen expects you to feel indignant at Mrs Norris's treatment of Fanny; Henry James expects you to feel indignant at Maisie's treatment at the hands of her parents; and George Eliot expects you to be gladdened that Dorothea, at a low point in her own fortunes, has the strength of mind to think of others.

8.3   Or you could put it another way: do the authors expect you to form *wishes*? Does Jane Austen expect you to *want* Fanny to be freed from oppression, and Turgenev expect you to *wish* that Insarov might not be doomed (as he so plainly is). I think you will agree that they do, and that this is the means by which they get you to make certain sorts of judgement for yourself.

Ask yourself, therefore: do you feel indignation, or gladness, or a wish that things could be different in reading *Anna Karenina*?

Discussion

8.4   Let us take indignation. Do you feel indignant, at Karenin's horrible letter to Anna? At Anna's neglect of her daughter? At Oblonsky's misdoings? For myself, I don't think that I do, or that I am meant to. Tolstoy *could* have made us indignant at these things with perfect ease, but it is not part of his plan to do so. Tolstoy places you, as a reader, at a point of vantage where you feel no wish that things should be different.

8.5   Does this mean that he is aloof and indifferent towards the fate of his characters —that he is treating them simply as a spectacle and intends us to do the same?

Discussion

8.6   I would say, not at all. He feels, and makes us feel, intensely for his characters, but this feeling is of a special kind: it is the feeling of kinship, of human solidarity, the sort of bond which unites the species and holds society together. He once wrote in his diary that 'The powerful means to true happiness in life, is to let flow from oneself on all sides, without any laws, like a spider, a cobweb of love, and to catch in it all that comes to hand: women old or young, children, or policemen'.[1] It is a good description of the way he writes; and this spider-like

---

[1] He made this diary-entry on 26 April 1856. (See Aylmer Maude's *Life of Tolstoy*, World's Classics ed., Dent, vol. 1, p. 151.)

MEALTIMES

The most important thing about mealtimes is that your child should come happily when you call out 'dinner time'. Battles over food can't always be avoided. But start on the positive side and look at some of the natural learning that can take place at mealtimes.

Getting to grips

In *Dressing* we looked at the difference between large movements and fine control of the hands and fingers. Most of the skills used at the table are fine control skills. Your child has to learn to make very 'neat' use of his hands and fingers.

Remember your baby's first attempts to feed herself – fingers into everything, food everywhere, followed by a battle over the spoon? By two she's probably managing a spoon quite well. But the fingers have a long way to go, from those early attempts, through the spoon stage, to getting a grown-up grasp on things.

Compare the way you and your child pick up and use the following objects.

Tick 'fist' if you use the whole hand, and 'finger' if you grip the object between your fingers and thumb in some way.

Fist grip on a spoon

Object	Your child		You	
	Fist	Finger	Fist	Finger
Spoon				
Fork				
Knife				
Cup				
Beaker				
Jug				

You'll probably find that your child makes greater use of his whole hand for holding these objects, while you tend to grip more with your fingers. To find out what this difference means, try holding a spoon in a fist grip and eating from it. You'll notice that you need to make much larger movements with your arm this way, it's less easy to control the spoon and harder to eat properly.

Helping messy eaters

We need to accept that small children are likely for a time to be messy eaters. Natural 'maturing' of the body will do most of the work for us. Finer movements will follow from the large arm movements and the first grip as the child's body becomes more physically able. It's the same as learning to walk – you can encourage a child when the time is right, but you can't make her walk before she's ready.

This doesn't mean you shouldn't give your child a knife and fork. Many children make rapid strides in self-feeding when given a set of their own cutlery. In addition you may be able to help by:

● providing a special small child-sized set of cutlery. You can buy spoons and forks with specially shaped handles – hold one to see the advantage for a fist-gripper.

● providing a dish with straight sides to push food against to get it on the spoon or fork more easily.

● providing toys such as simple jig-saws or shape-fitting boards which will give your child practice at grasping and handling small objects precisely.

● not worrying! Anxiety and constant comment on your part won't help. A very rough guide of what to expect at what age is given below – but as with all physical development children vary enormously.

At 2 years . . .
Uses a spoon well. May manage a fork. Can lift and put down a cup with two hands. May go back to fingers occasionally.

At 3 years . . .
Uses fork and spoon quite tidily. Can hold a cup with one hand.

At 4 years . . .
Uses knife, fork and spoon, though may need help with difficult cutting. Can serve himself from jugs and dishes.

Home Experiment 2

To do the experiment you will need the following items from your Home Experiment Kit, Part 2:

*Apparatus**

$100\,cm^3$ beaker

$100\,cm^3$ measuring cylinder

rack of test-tubes

$5\,cm^3$ syringe

2 dosing pipettes†

wash-bottle containing distilled water

spatula

Chemicals

sodium hydroxide

dilute hydrochloric acid (8.9%)

ferric nitrate (iron(III) nitrate)

potassium thiocyanate

Part 1

(a) Using your measuring cylinder, measure $50\,cm^3$ of distilled water into a beaker and add five pellets of sodium hydroxide, NaOH. Allow to dissolve.

(b) Add enough ferric nitrate, $Fe(NO_3)_3$, to a test-tube until the rounded bottom is full. Add enough distilled water to half-fill the test-tube, and shake until the solid dissolves.

(c) Add *one* crystal of potassium thiocyanate, KSCN, to a test-tube and add enough distilled water to half-fill it. Again shake to dissolve.

All three solutions are ionic. Note the colour of each solution and try to decide which ions are present: record these in Table 2.

TABLE 2   Observations for part 1 of Home Experiment 2

Solid	Colour of solution	Ions present
sodium hydroxide, NaOH		
ferric nitrate, $Fe(NO_3)_3$		
potassium thiocyanate, KSCN		

Now listen to the first part of the tape.

Extract from tape

"Now that you've prepared the three solutions, check your entries in Table 2. First, the columns: Both the sodium hydroxide and the potassium thiocyanate are colourless. But the ferric nitrate solution should be yellow. If you found any marked differences from these colours, you should make up that solution again, taking care that the test tube or flask is really clean—wash it well with distilled water before adding the chemical, and don't forget to wash and dry your spatula before using it.

Now what about the ions in these solutions? Well, you've already met sodium hydroxide, so I expect. . . "

The reception area

Start this section by carrying out the following activity which will help you assess what makes a good reception area.

ACTIVITY 7   Look at the following picture of a receptionist and reception area. This is not an ideal situation. What is wrong with it? Label the bad points shown in the picture.

Turn to page 36 for our assessment of this reception area. Look, too, at the picture on page 23 which offers a real contrast – a much more welcoming and attractive scene!

Part 5 Assessment Exercise

Part Five of the video, *Competence Assessment – Exercise*, shows the assessment of Andy, from Customer Service, while fitting Mr and Mrs Cartwright's fire.

Put yourself in the place of the assessor and observe Andy as he carries out the task you are assessing him on. This Element of Competence is 'Communicate with the Customer', a general task which many people in the Company perform.

This example should give you a flavour of the assessment process, rather than teach you specific assessment skills.

Before you watch the video, read the Performance Criteria on the facing page.

During Part Five you should tick any of these criteria which you observe Andy meeting. Put a cross against those criteria he does not meet, and leave blank where there is no evidence either way.

When you have completed watching Part Five you should compare your assessment form with the completed form on page 32.

Please note that some of the operational procedures in the video may differ from those in your region.

Now watch Part Five of the video,
Competence Assessment – Exercise.

(continued)

98 | As the officer in the case what observations would you have on the request to have his friend informed of his arrest?   **98**

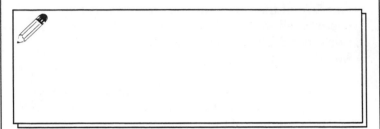

What options are open to you if you want to challenge this request?

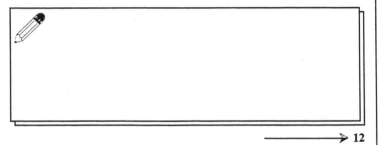

⟶ **12**

$\begin{smallmatrix}8\\40\end{smallmatrix}$ ⟶ **99** | In the current climate, it is important to recognise that admissions can still be rendered inadmissible if they are obtained in an improper manner. Secs 76, 77 and 78 PACE outline the law relating to confessions and the exclusion of unfair evidence.   **99**

What are you going to do now?

Charge immediately. ⟶ **2**

Obtain a witness statement from Mrs Woodhams. ⟶ **107**

Conduct a search of Wayne's home. ⟶ **46**

Check the location of the outstanding property. ⟶ **64**

NOTE: This sample is from a "branching" workbook, in which your decisions in response to key multiple-choice questions take you to different pages from other readers—and your investigation then develops differently from theirs.

Serving wine

The disadvantage of serving wines by the glass is that, once opened, they will not last. So establishments have to be sure, while extending their range, that the demand exists and wines will not go to waste. It is important therefore to make the customer aware of the range of wines that is available. Many establishments display notices to this effect, but staff can also help sales by telling customers what is on offer at the time the order is made

The need to display wines attractively in bars is probably more necessary than in restaurants where a wine list can be handed directly to the customer to show what is on offer. One solution is to place the whites and rosés in an ice bucket or special insulated holder on the bar counter or back fitting, and some red wines on racks clearly visible to the customer. Or white and rosé wine bottles can be placed in special cooling cabinets attached to measured dispensers. These cabinets are attached to the bar wall where they can be easily seen by customers

How wine is dispensed

Simply tilting the bottle into the glass is still the most common way of dispensing wine. Once the bottle is opened and exposed to the air, the wine soon becomes oxidised and undrinkable. With sales of wine by the glass, this would lead to a lot of wastage, but wine boxes, wine-cooling cabinets which dispense the wine through an optic or special wine measure, and wine-dispense systems which pump-up wine in pipes from a bulk container in the cellar, manage to solve the problem by preventing air from entering the wine as it is drawn off. Special bottle stoppers have also been developed to keep opened bottles of wine in good condition for longer than is possible with a plain cork.

Wine by the glass

Most licensees have adopted the code of practice on the sale of wine by the glass which stipulates the measures of still wines which can be served in a glass (see unit 2). It must be made clear, by a notice displayed where customers can see it, that the establishment has adopted the code. A variety of measures is allowed, both in imperial and metric, but the licensee must choose no more than two, both of which must be either metric or imperial measures differing from each other by at least 50 ml (2 fl oz). Many establishments choose to serve 125 ml because an exact number of glasses can be obtained from a 75 cl bottle.

         TO DO

Visit a licensed establishment of your choice and make notes on where (cellar/storeroom /cupboard/refrigerator/racks behind bar), at what temperatures and in what conditions (lying on their sides, upside down, upright on racks/shelves/in their original boxes) the different types of wine are stored (red/white/rosé/sparkling/boxed/screw top).

Then answer the following questions.
1. How many bottles of red wine are kept at room temperature and for how long before service? (The number of bottles may vary depending on the day of the week.)
2. How many bottles of white, rosé and sparkling wines are kept chilled, at what temperatures and for how long before service?
3. What is the average number of bottles of wine (red/white/rosé/sparkling) sold (a) on the busiest day, (b) on the quietest day?
4. From these figures, calculate the number each of red, white, rosé and sparkling wines brought to the correct serving temperature as reserves (in other words, will probably not be needed that day).

UNIT 4

THE INTERVIEW

Introduction

In this unit you will look at the art of effective interviewing. It sounds easy, but to be a good interviewer takes skill, self discipline and a knowledge of your own prejudices.

Purposes of this unit

When you have completed this unit you should be able to:

- create a suitable environment for an interview
- plan a structure for the discussion
- prepare individual questions based on the seven point plan
- take into consideration the importance of first impressions
- conduct the interview in such a way as to acquire the information needed to come to a fair decision
- close the interview effectively
- make a final decision and take appropriate follow-up action.

▮ Why interview?

Interviews are the most common and, sometimes, the sole method by which organisations assess a candidate's suitability for the job.

Since so much depends on these encounters, it is worth asking how effective they are as a means of selection.

What can interviews tell you about a candidate's ability to do a job? – and what can't they tell you? Write your ideas in the space below:

They can tell you	They cannot tell you ...
_____	_____
_____	_____
_____	_____
_____	_____

David, regional manager, clearing bank

'I'm very much in favour of interviews because you meet candidates face to face. I believe you can make an accurate judgement of their interpersonal skills and you have the chance to pose questions which can test this. The other factors are less tangible; you can get a sense of their enthusiasm – perhaps even their approach – and, most importantly, a sense of how much they want the job.'

Ronnie, distribution manager, sportswear manufacturer

'We use interviews almost exclusively – other methods are only used for top jobs. I think so much depends on the skills of the interviewer. The best interviewers can draw out much of the information they require, but most of us only interview sporadically. I've also found that interviews rarely help me to answer what for me is a big question: can they do the job in the way we want?'

Gwen, section head, petrochemical company

'My background is in personnel so I suppose I have a slightly different view of interviewing. I believe interviewing is the most effective way of selecting staff for most jobs but I feel it's very easy to have far too much faith in it as a single method. If there is no other method such as testing involved, always try to make sure that the application forms and preparatory work by selectors are as detailed as possible.'

Can you add anything else to the list as a result of what these managers described? After you have finished, compare your list with the one below.

They can tell you about:

- attributes such as appearance and manner

- motivation and how much the candidate wants the job

- interpersonal and communication skills

They can also ...

- enable the candidate to ask questions about the job

- give you the chance to find out more about specific points

They cannot tell you about:

- the candidate's practical skills

Other drawbacks ...

- inexperienced interviewers might not help the candidate to be seen in the best light

- interview nerves may inhibit an otherwise excellent candidate

Section 1:   Why trees and shrubs, and how to find out more about them

In this Section I'll look at why some gardeners prefer trees and shrubs to more formal garden designs. I'll also show you how to make a 'Looking good' list of plants for each month and how to collect information about each plant so that you can make sound recommendations to your customers.

Why choose trees and shrubs?

Many knowledgeable gardeners prefer to have borders that contain mixed shrubs rather than complex bedding designs and herbaceous borders. Why do you think this is? Try to think of 3 reasons and jot them down in the box below.

> 1.
>
> 2.
>
> 3.

You could have suggested any of the following reasons:

1.   Trees and shrubs offer an attractive, year-round display, with a variety of form, colour and height. The careful selection of plants will ensure:

   - something is in flower all year round (see the section in **Hillier's Manual of Trees & Shrubs**, page 567, and pages 33, 37 and 44 of **The Tree & Shrub Expert**)
   - a contrast of colour (variegated or evergreen leaves) and shape (bold-shaped foliage or fern-like leaves)
   - berries or stems for winter colour.

2.   A mixture of shrubs can cover the ground so as to suppress weed growth.

3.   Digging is unnecessary once trees and shrubs are established, and only light cultivation is needed. Read the articles on mulching and hoeing on page 107 of **The Tree & Shrub Expert**.

1: SOME IMPORTANT BUDDHIST TEACHINGS

The Four Noble Truths including The Eightfold Path

Do you remember *The Four Signs* (Religions page 195)? *Siddhartha Gautama* met four people and eventually came to *The Four Noble Truths.*

 READ Religions pages 198 - 201

and then...

 MAKE a dictionary list of the following:
    dukkha samudaya nirodha magga

 If possible look at the Buddhism in Focus 1 video.
LOOK at the picture of The Wheel of Life and read the accompanying explanation.

 If possible read Looking for Happiness pages 22 - 26.

 DESIGN a poster to show *The Eightfold Path.*
Try to make sure that it shows what each stage means.

The Five Precepts

A lay Buddhist lives by *5 basic rules* usually called *The Five Precepts.*

To find out about these:

 READ Religions pages 204 - 207

 WRITE out The Five Precepts.

 IN YOUR TUTORIAL discuss how your life would have to change if you became a Buddhist. Are there any parts of *The Four Noble Truths, Eightfold Path* or *Five Precepts* which you would find particularly attractive, difficult, or with which you would disagree?

BUDDHISM UNIT 3.2

53998

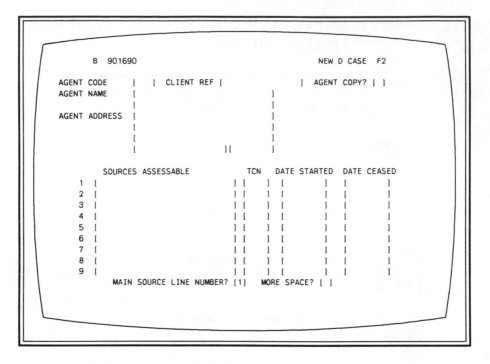

```
        B   901690                           NEW D CASE   F2

AGENT CODE     [   ]  CLIENT REF [                 ]  AGENT COPY? [ ]
AGENT NAME     [                             ]
               [                             ]
AGENT ADDRESS  [                             ]
               [                             ]
               [                    ] [      ]

          SOURCES  ASSESSABLE            TCN    DATE STARTED   DATE CEASED
       1 [                            ] [   ] [         ] [           ]
       2 [                            ] [   ] [         ] [           ]
       3 [                            ] [   ] [         ] [           ]
       4 [                            ] [   ] [         ] [           ]
       5 [                            ] [   ] [         ] [           ]
       6 [                            ] [   ] [         ] [           ]
       7 [                            ] [   ] [         ] [           ]
       8 [                            ] [   ] [         ] [           ]
       9 [                            ] [   ] [         ] [           ]
          MAIN  SOURCE  LINE  NUMBER? [1]   MORE SPACE? [ ]
```

Your screen now shows Format 2.

▶ Complete this screen

● Can you remember where to find the TCN? If not turn back to page 23

● Compare your completed screen with the next page
  before you press SEND

1 Introduction

Your project will be a very important part of your work on U206, indeed you may remember it vividly long after the other course materials have faded from your memory. The importance is not in terms of time spent – the project is only allocated 5 weeks and so must be small – but in the quality of the learning experience. In particular, your project will be a major part of achieving the third of the course aims – evaluating desirable courses of *action*. It would be improper for the course team to tell you how to act, or even that you should act, but we are asking you to develop skills by behaving as if you were going to act. We are asking you to investigate a local environmental issue, to write a short report and to draft a letter to an appropriate decision-making body advocating a particular outcome.

This task is intended to involve you in three ways which most of the course does not:

- the issue should be local, and preferably one where the outcome affects you directly
- we are asking you to draw on experience and skills which you already possess
- you will have to develop new skills of enquiry, interpretation and advocacy if you are to solve the problems you set yourself.

As a result of these factors, most students who do projects find that they generate much stronger feelings than the more passive learning elsewhere in the OU system. The job of this *Project Handbook* is to provide a framework to help you to take on this challenge successfully, so that you can emerge with strong *positive* feelings rather than the disappointment that can result when projects go wrong. We have written this booklet and scheduled feedback from your tutor to minimise the opportunities for error, but the nature of a project is that the ultimate responsibility is yours.

A word of warning is needed at this point: although the project will be yours and will be influenced by your values, there is no point in a piece of work which starts from your prejudices, selects information and views only if they accord with those prejudices and then attempts to hector decision-makers to accept them. What we hope you will achieve is an investigation which dispassionately seeks evidence and understanding and then uses that evidence, along with a justified set of values or goals, to argue for particular action.

To produce such a piece of work will be challenging, because it combines enquiry and self-analysis, but will be easier if you are sceptical about your own preferences as well as those of other people or groups who are involved. The issue of handling values as well as evidence is discussed at appropriate points in this booklet and links to Book One, Chapter 7.

1.1 Framework

The framework we are suggesting is one that divides your project work into four stages, each with assessment in a TMA and hence with tutor feedback. The stages are:

- choosing a topic   20% of
  TMA 01 (500 words max.)   mark
- planning your investigation 50% of
  TMA 03 (750 words max.)   mark
- collecting and interpreting
  information   50% of
  TMA 05 (1000 words max.)   mark
- reporting your findings
  TMA 07 (1600 words max.)   80% and
  plus recommendations for action 20% of
  (400 words max.)   mark

The suggested time allocations mean that about a third of your time should be devoted to each of planning, execution and report-writing. This is because careful planning is vital to success, and so is effective presentation.

1.2 Summary

To sum up the introduction, the project has the broad aim of carrying out an investigation of a local environmental issue and recommending action. To accomplish this you will have to achieve a number of linked objectives:

- develop skills in planning an investigation
- develop skills in finding out, i.e. gathering and interpreting information
- develop skills in report-writing.

Many of the particular ideas and skills needed for the project are used in course materials or taught through the other TMAs. It is the application of a wide range of ideas from the course to the particular project which justifies us in offering nearly a third of the continuous assessment marks for an activity which occupies less than a sixth of the course.

2 What kind of project?

By now you may be eager to get on with choosing a topic, but you may also be saying, 'I know what the objectives are and what the procedures look like but I don't know what you mean by a project.' So, before going on to discuss how *you* will choose (in Section 2.2), we are providing some examples which may give you a better 'feel' for what we

mean, as well as suggesting some possible 'ways in' to choosing.

There are several possible 'ways in' to choosing a topic. We have used three ways (and three authors) to demonstrate how you might go about making your choice: by your 'lifestyle'; by your 'surroundings'; by 'the media'. We know that choosing a theme may be the most difficult part of doing a project so these notes are intended to

Figure 4.9

Figure 4.10

Figure 4.11

Figure 4.12

Project 2: landscapes

[3 hours]

While buildings and views of towns and villages offer a wide range of locations and different subjects, for many it is a desire to make contact with nature that has encouraged them to draw in the first place. Drawing the landscape can be very rewarding. It was what the French painter Boudin (1824-1898) advised the Impressionists to do and which led to one of the most influential movements in the history of art. 'Study, learn to see and to paint, draw, paint landscapes. The sea and the sky are so beautiful - animals, people, trees just as nature has made them with their personalities, their real way of being in the air, in the light just as they are.'

I have used the word 'landscape' above but not as a generic term for hills, mountains and fields. I also include the smaller-scale landscapes in parks and gardens. A greenhouse can provide a kind of 'interior landscape' and even a window-box is a landscape in miniature.

You could make your landscape drawings from a window but if possible take Boudin's advice and work out in the open air. Parks are particularly good places to draw and they even provide seats!

Studies and a drawing

I want you to plan your work as I suggested you did in the last project. Again you should make at least 3 preliminary studies and then a drawing (A2 size if possible) on which you should spend at least 2 hours. Work in line and tone. Consider using different media from the ones you used in the last project. Try to make the longer drawing in a single session without a break. This may need some self-discipline as it is only too easy to decide that a break for a snack will be beneficial. It seldom is, because it is difficult to become immersed in the subject again even after a short break. I find that when I am drawing outside, it is better to plough on, without any stops until I have finished what I intended to do.

When you have completed this project pin up the work from it and the drawings from the last project and compare them.

WHAT HAVE YOU ACHIEVED?

Did you find that you used your experience from the townscape project when you drew your landscapes?

Which of the drawings or studies do you feel best captures the subject?

Have you been aware of making use of accidental effects in these drawings?

Did you find the shapes and forms of trees and plants more difficult to translate than the more clearly defined forms of buildings?

Are you still using the wide variety of marks you discovered in Chapter1?

It is likely that the trees and plants may have caused you problems. It can be extremely difficult to stop them looking like flat, cut-out shapes. You will find it useful to look at reproductions in books on drawing to see the many ways in which artists have translated landscape forms.

So far all your drawings have been direct translations of what you have seen. This has enabled you to make drawings which give a sense of three-dimensional form and depth. Creating an illusion of three-dimensions is the essence of drawing and as well as creating it by looking and selecting, there are a number of 'drawing systems' which produce an illusionary three-dimensional world on paper. In the next chapter you will be considering some of them.

Sending the assignment to your tutor

Now is again the time to send work to your tutor. Follow the same procedures as you did at the end of chapter 2. Don't wait for a response before continuing with the course.

ACTIVITY 30

start:

finish: —

TE TOCA A TI - NOW ITS YOUR TURN

a. Listen to the tape and imagine that you are the first 5 people from ACTIVITY 28 in turn and when asked these 4 questions.

> 1. *¿Cómo te llamas?*   2. *¿Cuántos anos tienes?*
>
> 3. *¿Dónde vives?*   4. *¿Tienes hermanos?*

Answer aloud in the pause for each person. The correct answer will be given to you after the pause. Start with Alicia.

b. Now imagine that you are the interviewer and ask the 5 students from ACTIVITY 28 the same 4 questions. Ask the questions aloud in order in the pause after the bleep and the students will give their answers.

> *Now I can ask a Spanish person if they have any brothers and sisters*

ACTIVITY 31

TE TOCA A TI - NOW ITS YOUR TURN

a. Now write the answer to the 4 questions about yourself:

> *¿Cómo te llamas?*   ....
>
> *¿Dónde vives?*   ....
>
> *¿Cuántos anos tienes?*   ....
>
> *¿Tienes hermanos?*   ....

b. Practise asking and answering these aloud or pair up with a friend to practise.

c. Then fill in a form for yourself.

7.

Nombre :
Edad   :
Pueblo :
Familia :

> *Now I can fill out a simple form asking my name, age and where I live*

Now try this out on yourself.

Activity 2: Practice in using a T framework

1. Consider your life at the moment and think of it in three areas
   a) WORK — how you spend your time, which may or may not be in a paid job
   b) RELATIONSHIPS — relationships you have with people in your life, outside and inside the family
   c) YOUR IDENTITY — you as an individual, who and what you are at this point in your life
2. Choose one area as a focus; they will overlap but it is helpful to concentrate on one — Ann's was work, though it involved her relationships and identity.
3. Record yourself under the headings of the T framework.
4. As you do it and read it over, does it clarify anything for you?
5. Try to share it with somebody who knows you well and see if it agrees with, or if it changes, their understanding of you.

Comment

Some students find this activity very useful for furthering their understanding of themselves; others find it difficult to do on themselves but easier to do on other people. Others, after trying it several times, don't find it useful at all, so, don't think you have to use it — the frameworks in this unit are suggestions for you to test and see if they increase your ability to help others, not straight-jackets! But do try them before you discard them.

The three areas I asked you to consider are useful ways of thinking about a client's concerns as they talk: where is the focus — on work, relationships or identity? As I said, they usually overlap, but these simple frameworks help you sort into manageable chunks the great mass of details clients sometimes bring. This sorting can help you to summarise and check out your understanding with the client. Here's another chance to try the T framework.

Activity 3: Using a T framework with a client

1. Select a client you are helping, or have helped, or somebody you know well and try writing out the T framework on that individual.
2. If you were going to do a session with them, what questions might the framework raise in your mind to 'explore' with them?

Comment

I hope you will try this out with clients when you get an opportunity. Some counsellors write up the framework and then use it to work with the client in a second session; others give it to clients as 'homework' to fill in themselves between sessions, others use it as a method of recording, to help them think about the clients and their needs — you may find other ways to use it.

Let's move on to another framework.

their needs they would like you to meet is an excellent way of providing a more effective service.

Sources of information: the patients themselves

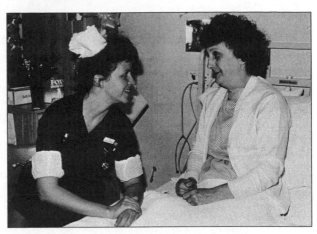

Activity 3.4

Select a maximum of four patients and ask them what they think their needs are. You may like to stick to the group of patients you are most involved with or go further afield and select a wider cross section. Whoever you decide to ask, work out a few questions in advance such as:

- What needs do you have that are being met by the NHS?
- What needs do you have that are **not** being met by the NHS?
- Which of these needs do you think are the most important?

1st patient	2nd patient	3rd patient	4th patient
1			
2			
3			
4			
5			
6			

Compare your original list of needs in Activity 3.2 with the patients' lists. Probably some needs appear in virtually all the lists while others appear only occasionally. Of course, much will depend on what sort of patients you asked, but you should be able to produce a new, expanded and, hopefully, fairly comprehensive list of patients' needs. Do this now on a separate sheet of paper.

Customer queries

You've almost completed this workbook on the Electrics department, and we hope you have enjoyed using it.

You can't expect to learn everything about electrics from just one workbook — but you should now know a lot more about the main aspects, especially safety.

There's just one more thing to do. We've covered a lot of information and some of it has been quite technical. Let's see now how much you will be able to help your customers with their queries on what they will need to do that electrical job.

Below, we've given a number of questions that customers might want advice on. What we want you to do is to write down how you would advise them. When you have answered the questions, take the workbook to your trainer who will go through them with you in detail.

Just a note of caution! You obviously can't claim to be an expert on electricity, so if you are in any doubt about the safety aspects of what a customer wants to do, refer them to your manager.

Question 1

' I want to move a light in my hallway. I've been told I need a junction box to extend the wiring, but I'm a bit confused by all the different sizes of wires. What should I use? '

Question 2

' I want to replace my mains fuses with minature circuit breakers. Will I need a new consumer unit? What size MCBS will I need? I've got 2 lighting circuits, 2 ring power circuits, and an immersion heater. '

Stage 1

Planning your materials

Route map for materials preparation

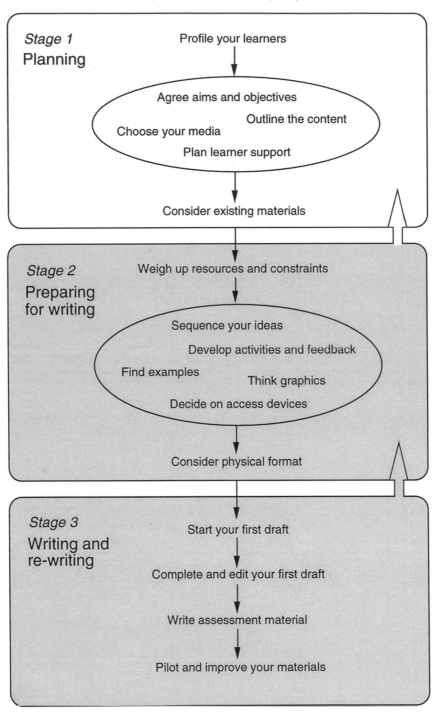

Stage 1
Planning

Profile your learners

Agree aims and objectives

Outline the content

Choose your media

Plan learner support

Consider existing materials

Stage 2
Preparing
for writing

Weigh up resources and constraints

Sequence your ideas

Develop activities and feedback

Find examples

Think graphics

Decide on access devices

Consider physical format

Stage 3
Writing and
re-writing

Start your first draft

Complete and edit your first draft

Write assessment material

Pilot and improve your materials

Task 1a
Profile your learners

How much do you know about your intending learners? If you are to provide effective open learning materials, you'll need to know quite a bit.

If you are preparing for learners you are already in touch with, you may know a lot to begin with. But perhaps you are preparing for learners you are not so familiar with. If so, there may be a great deal you need to find out about them.

The checklist overleaf may help you.

What do you need to know about your learners?

Demographic factors

☐ How many learners are you likely to have?

☐ How old?

☐ What sex and race?

☐ Any personal handicaps?

☐ Occupations (if any)?

☐ Whereabouts in (or out of) the country will they be learning?

Motivation

☐ Why are they learning?

☐ How might your programme relate to their lives or work?

☐ What do they want from the programme?

☐ What are their hopes and fears?

Learning factors

☐ What are their beliefs about learning?

☐ What learning styles do they prefer?

☐ What learning skills do they have?

☐ What experience of **open** learning?

Subject background

☐ How do they feel about the subject of the programme?

☐ What knowledge and skills do they already have in that subject?

☐ What misconceptions or inappropriate habits?

☐ What personal interests and experience might they have that are relevant?

Resource factors

☐ Where, when and how will they be learning?

☐ Who will be paying their fees or expenses?

☐ How much time will they have available?

☐ What access will they have to media/facilities?

☐ What access to human support—tutors, mentors, colleagues, other learners?

☐ *Other factors? (What?)*

How to find out?

So what do you already know about your intended learners that might be relevant to how you'll design the materials? What might you still need to find out about them?

And how might you set about obtaining the information you'll need? For instance, you might:

- Reflect on your previous experience of your learners, or broadly similar ones.

- Consult colleagues—and the learners' sponsors or your clients, if appropriate.

- Meet some of the prospective learners and discuss with them (individually or as a group) what they would like from the course or programme, and what they already know/feel about the subject.

- Send a questionnaire to prospective learners, trying to elicit the information you need. If this can be followed up by discussion with learners, whether face-to-face or on the telephone, so much the better.

- Keep in touch with your learners—e.g. by telephone, by meetings, or by reading and commenting on their assignments—once they are working on your materials.

Perhaps you'll be able to picture your learners or write a brief profile as I do on the next two pages.

Maybe you can then go on to draw up an "implications list" like the one I've set out on page 46.

Picturing our learners

Applicants for a "Women into Management" programme

*How shall we cater for the **diversity** among our learners?*

Profile of the typical learner
—for *"Managing your Farm's Finances"*

Our typical* learner runs a small farm or market garden.
He is male, between 30 and 40 years of age, and is
married with one or two children living at home. He
left school at 16 with a few examination certificates
and has done no systematic studying since. His most
regular reading will be at *Daily Mail* level.

He will not be worried about the cost of books or
travelling to course meetings and will be ready to obtain
playback machines for audio- and video-cassettes if he
does not have them already. However, he is unwilling
to commit himself to attending even occasional class
meetings at a fixed time (because of the unpredictable
demands of his work). This, in fact, is why he is
choosing an open learning course.

He is enrolling for the course in hope of improving his
efficiency and profitability and avoiding hassle from his
bank manager, accountant and tax inspector. He will be
perfectly capable of learning on his own, provided the
materials are flexible enough for him to find his own
level and he is allowed fairly ready access (at least by
telephone) to a tutor or other learners if he gets into
difficulties. The tutor will need to be scrupulous in
providing support rather than criticism.

Needless to say, the learner is very familiar with the
subject-matter of the course. He will be scathing about
anything he regards as "unrealistic" in our examples or
suggestions, and will not stick with the course unless it
remains clearly relevant to what he perceives as his needs.

** NOTE: Don't expect all learners to be typical
—e.g., a **few** of those "he"s may be "she"s!*

Knowing my learners—some implications

An example

My learners . . .	So I must . . .
are paying for the package themselves	try to avoid expensive media
have a fixed amount of time available for studying the package	be strict about how much material I include
will not see any obvious reason why they should study the package	emphasize how the package might benefit them (e.g. in their work)
have considerable experience in the subject covered by the package	appeal to that experience —e.g. by using examples suggested by learners
differ from me in the way they use certain key terms and ideas	begin by laying bare and exploring our differences
are chiefly readers of the *Sun* or *Mirror*	keep words, sentences and paragraphs short
are chiefly men but some will be women	try to make my language and examples equally welcoming to both sexes
may not be aware when the package has become relevant to their needs	persuade line managers to introduce the package to learners at the appropriate time

AND SO ON . . .

Development activities

1   If you'd like more ideas about
    relevant learner characteristics
    to look out for, read:

    • EXPLODL (pages 37–53)

    • MORGAN (1993)
      (chapters 1–4).

                    Then:

2   Decide what you'd like to find
    out about YOUR learners.

3   Use whatever combination of
    the five ways mentioned on page
    43 will best help you find out.

4   Draw up a profile and/or
    implications list showing the
    main characteristics of your
    learners that are likely to
    influence your materials.
    (Remember to note any
    important differences between
    learners as well as the things
    they have in common.)

5   Discuss your profile and/or
    implications list with a colleague
    and one or two of your intended
    learners. (The checklist overleaf
    may be useful in this.)

6   Revise your ideas as necessary
    in the light of the feedback you
    get.

Checklist

- Have you been able to collect all the information you'd like under the six headings on page 42? (If not, how might you obtain more?)

- Do other people agree with what you see as the likely characteristics of the learners? (If you don't get agreement, what might you need to do?)

- What problems and opportunities will these learner characteristics present you with in providing appropriate materials? (Or in providing human support for learners?)

- Do other people agree with what you see as the implications for the kind of materials you'll need to provide for learners?

- Are you clear about the prior knowledge and skills you are expecting learners to bring to the materials? (Will you need to pre-test learners and cater for them separately if they do not have the expected competences?)

- Have you made a note of any important ways in which your likely learners may differ from one another?

- How might you make it possible for different learners to use the materials differently to suit their individual needs?

- Can you see ways (e.g. through assignments) by which you or colleagues might find out how learners are coping with your materials—and perhaps adapt the teaching more closely to each individual's needs and interests?

Be alert to modify your picture of the learners—and the kind of teaching they need—as you get to know them better.

Task 1b
Agree aims and objectives

Objectives play a big part in open learning. They tell learners what they might get out of our materials. And they help us decide what to put into those materials.

Aims v objectives?

Some people are not too sure of the difference. And indeed both words are used rather loosely, along with others like goals, purposes and intentions—not to mention outcomes and competences. The displays on page 50 and 51 should help makes things clearer.

What kinds of objective?

The display on page 52 suggests that you and your learners may have several different kinds of objective.

Where are they to come from?

- You may be able to think up your own, perhaps by brainstorming with colleagues.

- You may be presented with them—e.g. by a client or curriculum document prepared by other people.

- You may need to arrive at them by observing skilled people doing their work or by studying published "standards of competence".

- You may also want learners to help decide the objectives.

Objectives v aims

AIMS   A **general** statement of EITHER

(a) what the learner might learn OR

(b) of what the teacher will do.

OBJECTIVES   A more **specific** statement about what the
learner will be able to **DO** (or do better) as a result.

Example—from a course on "Diet and Nutrition"

AIMS   "To learn about healthy eating habits" OR

"To introduce the learner to healthy eating habits"

OBJECTIVES   "The learner should be able to:

1. List the principal components of a
   balanced diet.

2. Describe the function of each in the body.

3. Calculate the composition of a given
   diet using food composition tables.

4. Suggest ways of improving his or her diet.

5. ... etc"

*BEWARE: Some published materials display so-called
objectives that are really more like aims. And some
use words and phrases like "Purposes", "Goals",
"What you will learn" or "Intended outcomes" as
a heading for what are clearly objectives.*

Sample aims and objectives
from three different courses

AIMS: To explain the concept and importance of energy; to provide practice in carrying out surveys and experiments relating to energy studies; to engender a sense of concern about the depletion of fossil fuel reserves; and to give the learner guidance on the planning of an energy policy.

OBJECTIVES: *The learner should be able to*:
1. List the various forms of energy
2. Describe how one form may be converted into another.
3. Distinguish between energy and power.
4. Identify the principal energy flows in a given situation.
5. ... etc.

§§§

AIMS: To help the non-financial manager use financial information in planning, controlling and making decisions.

OBJECTIVES: *The learner should be better able to*:
1. Construct and use a cash flow forecast.
2. Construct and use a profit and loss account.
3. Interpret a balance sheet.
4. Describe ways of recording and classifying expenditure.
5. Use specific budgets for planning and controlling.
6. ... etc.

§§§

AIMS: To foster an appreciation of the novels of D.H. Lawrence.

OBJECTIVES: *The learner should be able to:*
1. Relate Lawrence's viewpoint to his/her own experience.
2. Analyse the literary elements that have provoked his/her involvement.
3. Make and justify a personal statement as to Lawrence's "meanings".
4. Seek out and read more of Lawrence's writings than are set for assignments.
5. ... etc.

Four types of objective
MAUD—*a useful acronym*

M = Memory
e.g. Which terms, definitions, procedures, etc might the learner need to remember?

A = Attitudes
e.g. In what ways might we expect to see a shift in the learner's beliefs, values, concerns?

U = Understanding
e.g. In what new respects might learners be expected to explain, interpret or predict their world?

D = Doing
e.g. What new physical or interpersonal activities might learners become capable of carrying out?

Examples from the training of managers

Memory:
"The manager should be able to list Handy's eight causes of conflict."

Attitudes:
"The manager should demonstrate a desire to resolve conflicts within his/her own work-group in a way that satisfies all parties involved."

Understanding:
"The manager should be able to explain conflicts within his/her own work-group in terms of Handy's typology."

Doing:
"the manager should be able to uncover suppressed conflicts by means of sensitive interviewing."

(This last objective is primarily about an interpersonal skill, but it will involve M-A-U aspects as well.)

How to phrase objectives

Start your list with a statement such as:

> *"After you have worked through this
> (unit/pack/course, etc) you will be able
> (or be better able) to . . ."*

*and then list your objectives, each one beginning with a
verb whose performance can be **observed**. (For example,
could you sensibly say "Watch me . . ." or "Listen to me . . ."
before each objective?)*

AVOID words and phrases like:	*PREFER words and phrases like:*
know . . .	state . . .
understand . . .	describe . . .
really know . . .	give examples of . . .
fully understand . . .	suggest reasons why . . .
be familiar with . . .	explain . . .
become acquainted with . . .	evaluate . . .
have a good grasp of . . .	pick out . . .
gain a working knowledge of . . .	distinguish between . . .
appreciate . . .	analyse . . .
acquire a feeling for . . .	carry out . . .
realize the significance of . . .	summarize
be aware of . . .	show diagrammatically . . .
learn the basics of . . .	compare . . .
believe in . . .	demonstrate . . .
Others? (What?)	*Others? (What?)*

*It's OK to start with thoughts of "knowledge" or "understanding"
—but then ask yourself how you'd get the learner to demonstrate it.*

Overall objectives v sub-objectives

*You may find it useful to think in terms of "overall objectives" and "sub-objectives". Indeed, this will probably be **essential** if you are planning to write material for more than a few hours of learning time. For example, from a course on designing an open learning scheme:*

Course objectives ("overall objectives")

When you have worked through this course, you should be better able to:

1. Describe the main components needed in an open learning scheme and the roles played by each.
2. Give examples of different forms of open learning scheme.
3. Select and adapt open learning materials.
4. Identify the needs and characteristics of open learners.
5. Plan a learner support system.
6. Draw up a realistic budget for an open learning scheme.
7. Identify the key management issues in running the scheme.
8. Evaluate an open learning scheme.
9. Explain and justify your own vision of open learning.

Objectives of Units 3 and 6 ("sub-objectives")

Unit 3—As a result of working on this unit you could be better able to:

- Identify some of the reasons why your learners may need support.
- List some of the types of support they might be given—before, during and after their learning programme.
- Suggest people who might provide such support.
- Outline a plan for the selection and/or briefing and training of supporters.
- Decide how your supporters will be monitored and provided with back-up.

These sub-objectives relate chiefly to course objectives 5 and 7.

Unit 6—As a result of working on this unit you could be better able to:

- Give examples of learner costs and system costs.
- Decide what kind of costing you may need to carry out.
- Identify the costs involved in producing, delivering and sponsoring open learning.
- Show how the balance between fixed costs and variable costs and between cash costs and non-cash (hidden) costs affect a particular open learning project.

These sub-objectives relate chiefly to course objectives 6 and 8.

Development activities

1   If you'd like more ideas about developing aims and objectives, read:

    • TTSI (pages 43–47)

    • MAGER (1990).

            Then:

2   Write down the aims of your materials (just a sentence or two).

3   Head a sheet of paper with the statement:

    'After working through these materials, learners should be able to (or be better able to) . . .'

    and follow it with your list of learning objectives. (NOTE: If this is your first attempt at writing learning materials, you may find it easier to begin by planning for a unit or module, etc rather than for a whole course or programme.)

4   Discuss your objectives with colleagues and, if possible, with learners. (The checklist overleaf may be useful in this.)

5   Revise your ideas as necessary in the light of your feedback.

Checklist

- Have you been able to state some aims that make clear how learners might expect to benefit from the materials —e.g. in terms of competence at work or improved quality of life?

- Do your objectives have some obvious relation to the aims?

- Have the objectives you've written taken account of what learners say they'd want out of working with the materials?

- Are colleagues, clients and other "interested parties" agreed that these are the appropriate objectives?

- Are your objectives written in "watch me . . . /listen to me . . ." terms?

- If you are planning to provide for more than a few hours of learning time, have you tried to distinguish between overall objectives and sub-objectives? (See page 54.)

- Do your objectives cover all the essential knowledge, skills and attitudes that you are hoping learners will develop?

- Is it realistic to expect so much of them in the time they'll have available for working with your materials?

- Is it realistic to expect so much from **you** in the time you will have available for preparing those materials?

> *Be ready to develop your objectives further as you get ahead with your planning—e.g. as a result of tackling Task 1c.*

Task 1c

Outline the content

If you have already carried out Task 1b, you'll have a good idea what learners should be able to **do** as a result of working on your materials. You know where you want them to get to. But what sort of subject content might they need to work on along the way?

What are your main themes, issues and topics? What theories, principles or procedures might you need to explore?

Ways of thinking up content

There are many ways of deciding on content—apart from having a syllabus thrown at you and being told to get on with it. I've listed a few worth thinking about on page 59.

Research

This is the point at which one often needs to start researching the subject one is teaching. Clearly this will be necessary if you have been commissioned to prepare materials for a subject that is new to you. What do your clients want?

You may not think it necessary if you are preparing materials for a subject you have been teaching for some time. But, in my experience, the knowledge with which I felt comfortable enough in classroom teaching always seems to need refreshing before I feel equally comfortable recording my ideas in print. How about you?

My approach?

My own approach to content varies according to whether I am aiming chiefly to help learners:

(a)   Come to **see** their world differently or

(b)   Get to **act** differently on that world.

(This "world" might be the world of work, of an academic discipline, of personal relationships, or whatever.)

In the case of (a) I am likely to start by thinking about subject-matter. I will mostly use approaches from the left-hand list on page 59. In the case of (b) I will probably start with objectives and competences—and I'll certainly use more approaches from the right-hand list.

But few learning programmes are entirely (a) or entirely (b)—so I nearly always need to use approaches from both lists.

For instance, I may use brainstorming to come up with a deluge of ideas I might need to cover in my materials. (See pages 60 and 61.) But I probably can't get much further without thinking about the learners and what they might need to do with those ideas. Only then do I begin to see how the material might be structured.

Two sets of approaches to content

Subject-centred

- Review your own knowledge of the proposed subject—by personal brainstorming, making lists, diagrams, etc...

- Discuss the subject-area with experts/clients—e.g. through interviews or group brainstorming.

- Read existing materials pitched at what you regard as your learners' level.

- Read more advanced material on subject.

- Review films, video and audiotapes, and articles in newspapers and popular magazines.

- Analyse courses and packages on similar subjects.

- Study any relevant exam syllabus and question papers from past.

- Examine documents (books or other source materials) around which the learning could or must be organized.

- Identify and analyse the key concepts and principles of the subject.

o   *Any others? (What?)*

Learner-centred

- Ask prospective learners what topics/issues they would like to see tackled.

- Discuss with prospective learners their existing understandings and feelings about the key concepts of the subject-area.

- Analyse the knowledge, skills and attitudes displayed by "master performers"—or at least by "acceptably competent" performers.

- Recall or enquire where previous learners have had difficulties or fallen into error in the subject.

- Think of learning activities that learners logically must (or just usefully could) engage in.

- Consider how learners' development or attainments as a result of the learning might sensibly be assessed.

- Study other people's reports of learners' work on related courses in previous years.

- Establish and analyse the aims and learning objectives.

o   *Any others? (What?)*

You may choose to use some approaches from both lists

Initial brainstorm for a course
on open and distance learning

A page from my notepad showing my first thoughts about possible contents. (For greater flexibility, it may be better to write on a whiteboard or to use "post-it" stickers which can easily be moved around on a wall— especially if you are brainstorming with colleagues.)

Further brainstorms for detailed content

*Showing how each of the major topics in the initial sketch
needed to be brainstormed in greater detail. How far do you go?*

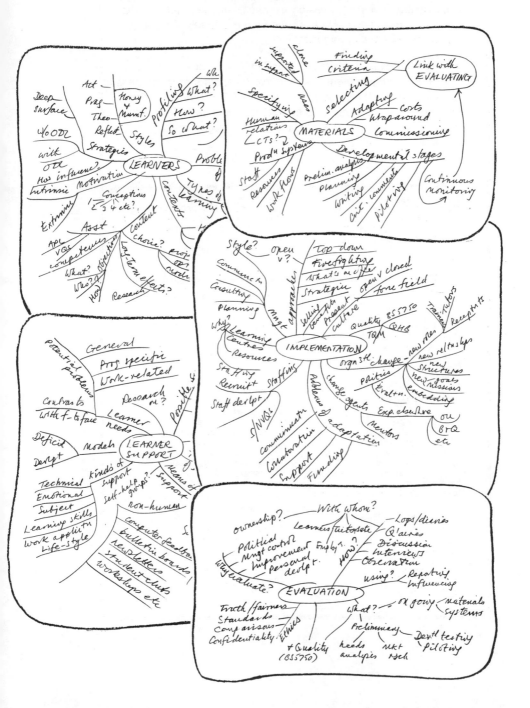

A draft contents outline

You may find it helpful—possibly essential—to make a list of the topics you might cover. Here is mine for the course I wrote about "Open and Distance Learning".

Most but not all of these topics found their way into the eventual course. But many of them "jumped" into units other than the ones suggested here. In fact, Unit 1 disappeared, Unit 3 became two separate units and I made up an additional unit out of important bits and pieces that seemed to belong better together than spread about elsewhere.

Unit 1—The history of OL

The autodidact in history
The role of the printed word
Correspondence courses
Programmed learning
Resource-based learning
The Open University
Open Tech

Unit 2—What is open and
            distance learning?

Different forms of open and
  distance learning
Definitions
What can be learned?
Education and training
Benefits
Weaknesses and dangers
Future trends

Unit 3—Learners and their
            support

Learner-centredness
Learners' orientations,
  beliefs, styles, etc
Finding out about learners
What will they learn?
Fostering learner autonomy
The need for support
Ways of providing support

Unit 4—Media in OL

What media are available?
Media case studies
Pros and cons of different
  media
How to choose
Ways of using media
Combining media

Unit 5—The package in OL

Forms of packages
The role of the package
Analysing materials
Evaluating existing packages
Ways of developing packages
Roles in package development

Unit 6—Costing OL

Why costing is important
Open v conventional costs
Hidden costs
Estimating your costs
Producers and deliverers
Learners' costs
Creative accounting
Sources of funding

Unit 7—Evaluating OL

What is evaluation?
Why bother to evaluate?
Theory of evaluation
Quality assurance
What needs evaluating?
Ways of evaluating
The reflective practitioner
Using evaluation results
Managing evaluation

Unit 8—Implementing OL

Open learning and change
Driving and restraining forces
Managing change
Staff development
Budgeting
Communication
Open management
Quality systems
Action plans

Development activities

1   If you'd like more ideas about ways of thinking up possible content for your materials, read:

   * TTSI (pages 48–60)
   * DCfS (Chapter 2).

   Then:

2   Use whatever methods suit you best to make a list or draw a map of the main topics that must be dealt with in your materials.

3   If you haven't shared your ideas with colleagues in the process of developing them, discuss your contents list now with colleagues, with subject-experts and, if practicable, with some learners.

4   Amend your list as necessary in the light of the discussion.

Checklist

- Are you satisfied that your contents cover everything necessary for a balanced and up-to-date treatment of the subject? (If not, what do you need to do next—e.g. more research, more consultations, more brainstorming?)

- Is it realistic to expect learners to be able to do justice to all the proposed content in the time they'll have available for these materials? If not, what can you cut out?

- Do other people agree with you about the content of the materials? (If you haven't yet got agreement, what might you need to do next—e.g. more discussions?)

- If you've already tackled Task 1b, does your proposed content cover everything necessary for learners to attain the objectives?

- Are there any areas of the proposed content that may seem irrelevant to certain learners (or to other interested parties, e.g. their employers)? If so, what might you need to do about this?

- Might it be worth giving learners some freedom to choose content? For example, might different learners choose to concentrate on different sections of the materials, and ignore others? Might they be able to suggest additional topics of their own—e.g. in assignments or projects?

- Do you see any potential problems (for you or for learners) in tackling any of the content? If so, it's not too soon to start thinking about how you might overcome them.

If you haven't already tackled Task 1b, now would be a good time to do so. Thinking about objectives can often suggest changes in content.

Task 1d

Choose your media

If you've tackled tasks 1a, 1b and 1c, you'll know who your materials are for, what your learners are meant to get out of them and what topics are to be covered. But what teaching or learning media should they involve?

What media are available?

Media are your ways and means of facilitating learning. Page 66 shows the variety of media available in open, distance or flexible learning. Basically, that's all the media commonly used in "conventional" learning plus a few that aren't.

How will you choose?

Page 67 suggests some of the criteria you might want to consider. Choosing may not be easy. You may find there are conflicts—e.g. between what your learners would most benefit from and what you can afford or have the skills to provide. Perhaps the most useful question to ask is:

What is the simplest/cheapest medium (or mix of media) that will satisfactorily (even if not perfectly) meet our learners' needs?

Try to AVOID being forced to:

- Decide on a medium before you've thought through your learners' needs and the objectives/content of the teaching.

- Use a medium simply because it's available or urged upon you by someone else.

- Go for a high-tech ("powerful") medium in the belief that it will automatically be more effective than a simpler one.

Some of the media available in open learning

Print-based

- Books, pamphlets, etc—already published, or specially written
- Study guides specially written to "wrap around" already published material
- Specially written self-teaching texts, e.g. "tutorials-in-print"
- Workbooks for use along with audiotape or videotape, CBT, practical work, etc
- Self-tests, project guides, notes on accreditation requirements, bibliographies, etc
- Maps, charts, photographs, posters, etc
- Material from newspapers, journals and periodicals
- Handwritten materials passing between learners and tutor.

Audio-visual or technology-based

- Audio-cassettes/discs/CDs
- Radio broadcasts
- Slides or filmstrip
- Film or film loops
- Video-cassettes
- Television broadcasts
- CBT or multi-media
- Interactive video.

Practical or project work

- Materials, equipment, specimens for learner's own use—e.g. home experiment kits, keyboards, official forms

- Field-work or other use of learner's local environment—e.g. observation, interviews, collection of evidence, etc
- Projects in local offices, farms, workshops, etc
- Assignments based on learner's workplace

Human interaction

At-a-distance

- Telephone conversation between learner and tutor (supplementing written communications)
- Learner–learner telephone conversations
- Several learners in telephone contact at the same time, with or without a tutor, by means of a "conference call"
- Video conferencing
- Computer conferencing.

Face-to-face

- Learners' self-help groups
- Help from colleagues/line managers/"mentors"/technicians
- Seminars, tutorials, lectures by tutors or other group organizers
- One-day, one week, weekend, or other short group sessions (residential or otherwise).

o *Others? (What?)*

How to choose your media

Some possible criteria

1 Do any of the learning objectives dictate certain media?

2 Which media will be physically available to the learners?

3 Which media will be most convenient for the learners to use?

4 Are any media likely to be particularly helpful in motivating learners?

5 Are you under pressure from the organization to use/avoid certain media?

6 Which media will you (the teacher/trainer) be most comfortable with?

7 Which media will learners already have the necessary skills to use?

8 Which media do you (the teacher/trainer) have the necessary skills to use?

9 Which media will you be able to afford to use?

10 Which media will the learners be able to afford to use?

11 Which media might you call on to back up the main media and/or to ensure adequate variety?

o *Other criteria peculiar to your circumstances? . . .*

Which criteria are most important to you?

Which media might best do what?

*The chart below lists some things you might want to do with your media—and suggests which of the more common media might **best** enable you to do each one.*

Some possible media ➜

Things you might want to do in your teaching	Print	Audio	Video	Interactive video	Practical work	Computer tutoring	Computer simulation	Multi-media	Computer conferencing	Lecturing	Face-to-face tutoring	Telephone tutoring	Correspondence tutoring
Provide a carefully-argued analysis of your subject.	✓	✓								✓			
Convey the sights, sounds and spirit of your subject.		✓	✓	✓	✓		✓	✓					
Build each learner's ideas into the teaching.						✓			✓		✓	✓	✓
Ask learners to answer questions about the subject.	✓	✓	✓	✓		✓		✓	✓		✓	✓	✓
Enable learners to try things out, physically.					✓		✓						
Ensure that learners get physical feedback from the real world.					✓		✓						
Give learners standardized verbal feedback according to what category of response they make.	✓	✓		✓		✓		✓					
Give each learner unique, personal feedback.									✓		✓	✓	✓
Continuously alter the teaching to suit each learner's current needs.											✓	✓	✓
Provide learners with a record of the learning experience.	✓												
Others? (What?)													

*So—which **combination** of media might best suit YOUR needs?*

Development activities

1 If you'd like more ideas about choice of media, read:

- TTSI (chapter 11)
- EXPLODL (pages 95–119)
- LAURILLARD (1993) (chapters 5–9)
- LEWIS & PAINE (1986) (pages 69–101).

Then:

2 Decide which of your content and objectives can be dealt with well enough by printed material—and which may need (or at least benefit from) audio, video, CBT, practical work or interaction with other people.

3 Write yourself a memo saying which media you have chosen and what is to be the special role of each. (For example, what 'added value' might you be hoping for from video or CBT over and above what you might get from print alone?)

4 Discuss your memo with one or more colleagues (including a media specialist if possible).

5 Revise your ideas as necessary in the light of the feedback you get.

Checklist

- Have you been able to argue a convincing case for your choice of media? (Consider drawing up a chart along the lines of that shown on page 68.)

- Have you considered how media might be **combined**—e.g. print plus audio, or class sessions with pre-read material?

- Are you sure you have the know-how (or can get it soon enough) to make worthwhile use of your chosen media?

- Are you happy that you will have enough personal control over your media—i.e. not be more dependent than you'd like on media professionals?

- Will your learners be able to use your chosen media conveniently and without undue cost to themselves?

- Will your learners have positive feelings about your chosen media—and the learning skills to use them?

- If you plan to use non-print media, have you considered how printed material might be used in support?

- If you plan to use "human media"—tutors, line managers and other supporters—are you confident that suitable people will be available and willing to help?

- If you plan to have your learners do practical work, carry out workplace activities, or pursue projects in the "real world", can you see how to ensure they can do so conveniently, effectively and safely?

- Are you sure that your choice of media will not require you to cut back (e.g. on the grounds of cost or time) on some other, more desirable, aspect of what you might provide for learners?

- Have you avoided the three dangers mentioned at the foot of page 65?

No one medium is ideal for all purposes. But any medium used with imagination can be very effective for most.

Task 1e

Plan for learner support

Materials are usually important in open, distance and flexible learning. But they are not all-important. In fact, they are not usually much use on their own.

Unless your learners are supported by the right kind of interest and help from other human beings, they may not learn as much as you'd hope from your materials.

If you have worked on Task 1d, you may already have started thinking about "human media". Indeed, you may be planning to support your learners yourself. Some other possible supporters are listed on page 74.

Even if it's not your job . . .

On the other hand, it may not be your job to decide how your learners should be supported. Or to decide who might provide such support. All the same, you do need to think about it.

- For one thing, it may influence the way you write your materials—e.g. is there anyone available to comment on any exercises you may plan to set the learner?

- And for another, if learners don't get the kind of support they need when using your materials, their failures may be blamed on your materials (and on you).

So you may want to make some suggestions to whoever is responsible for organizing support—either by briefing them personally or by providing a "Supporter's Guide" along with your materials.

What might supporters do?

If you have already tackled Task 1a, you may have a good idea
of the kinds of help and support your learners are likely to
need. Most learners will need someone who can respond to
them as **individuals**—someone who can respond to each
learner's personal needs and concerns.

The opposite page lists some of the many kinds of help that
different supporters might be asked to provide.

Kinds of help your supporters might need to provide

1   Provide entry and exit counselling to learners.

2   Help learners select appropriate learning materials.

3   Adapt learning materials to suit the needs of an individual learner.

4   Agree a plan of support with individual learners.

5   Assess learners' progress at intervals and give them helpful feedback.

6   Offer general guidance about approaches to learning.

7   Give individual learners help with specific learning difficulties.

8   Comment on materials produced by learners in response to exercises, activities, assignments, etc.

9   Help learners widen or deepen their understanding.

10   Coach or counsel learners, individually, on the phone or face-to-face.

11   Run group sessions for learners.

12   Help learners get support from other people (e.g. at their workplace).

13   Help learners apply what they are learning to their jobs.

14   Keep records of learners' progress.

15   Assess learners' knowledge and understanding.

16   Assess learners' practical competence.

17   Manage physical resources for a learning programme.

18   Provide data towards evaluation of materials and systems.

o   *Others? (What?)*

Some possible supporters

*Here are the kinds of people who may have
a part to play in helping your learners*

☐ an adviser or counsellor

☐ a tutor

☐ a mentor

☐ the learners' line managers

☐ technicians or demonstrators

☐ librarians

☐ learning centre receptionists

☐ other learners

☐ friends, family, colleagues, etc

☐ *Others? (Who?)*

*Can you identify any such people in your
organization (or elswhere) who might take up
some of the roles mentioned on the page 73?
(Which people, and which roles?)*

Development activities

1 If you'd like more ideas about supporting open learners, read:

   • EXPLODL (pages 71–93).

   Then:

2 Decide, possibly with the help of some learners, what kinds of support your learners might need.

3 Consider, preferably with the help of colleagues, who might meet those needs—in what ways and to what extent.

4 Check out the feasibility of such types and levels of support with whoever would need to provide the necessary resources.

5 Take note of the types and level of support you'll be able to assume your learners will get. (You may want to refer to it in your materials.

Checklist

- Have you used what you know of learners (see Task 1a) to plan what kinds of individual help and support they might need?

- Have you been able to identify people who might provide this help and support?

- If not, how might appropriate people be recruited (or persuaded) to take on full-time or part-time support duties?

- Have you decided what roles each person might need to play in providing support?

- What new knowledge, skills and attitudes might those people need in their role as supporters?

- How might appropriate training, staff development and support be provided for the supporters?

- What briefing materials might you need to prepare for supporters if they are to know how best to play their part?

- How might the work of supporters be monitored and "best practice" made more widespread?

- Have you identified any support roles for learners themselves—e.g. in supporting one another as members of self-help groups or in carrying out group activities?

- Given the kind and level of support that might be available for your learners, how does this affect the kind of learning materials you will provide for them?

- Have you asked any potential learners whether what you have in mind is the kind of support they'd be hoping for?

> Only the 'human media' (supporters) can respond personally to the individual needs of your learners.

Task 1f

Consider existing material

So, can we say you've now carried out tasks 1a–e? If so:

- You'll have a pretty clear idea of the kind of materials your learners will need.
- You'll know what the objectives should be.
- You'll know the main content that must be included.
- You'll have decided which media and methods are most appropriate.
- You'll have given some thought to the level of human support that might be needed by learners using the materials.

Now you need to brace yourself for writing those materials, right? Well, perhaps not. Huge quantities of teaching and learning material are already in existence. Maybe you can use some of it—and save yourself a lot of time, money and hassle.

Your three main options

When preparing open learning materials, you have three main options:

- Use existing open learning materials—with or without additional new material of your own.

- Build on existing **non**-open learning material (e.g. textbooks or videos or government pamphlets)

- Plan and develop your own custom-made materials from scratch.

Think twice before assuming you must have all your materials custom-made. You **may** be able to meet at least some of your learners' needs with materials that exist already. If so, you may save hugely on time, money and hassle.

Using existing open learning materials

The opposite page lists several possible sources of existing open learning materials. You may also know of other organizations like your own that have been producing open learning materials.

• Have any of them got materials that fit your specification? (Evaluate them using criteria like those on page 82.)

• If so, could you (and your learners) afford to use them?

• If they are almost OK, could you make them usable by preparing a separate study guide? This might tell learners which bits of the materials to ignore, provide alternative examples, additional material, and so on.

• If they are not quite that OK, could you get permission to alter (and reprint) them to suit your requirements?

Copyright

If you wish to alter (and reprint) other people's materials to better suit your requirements, you will need copyright permission. This could be expensive—but it might still be cheaper than producing your own from scratch.

Sources to contact about existing open learning materials you might use

- International Centre for
    Distance Learning
  The Open University
  Milton Keynes MK7 6AA
  (Tel: 0908-653537)
  *Documentation centre on
  distance education worldwide.
  Its database (available on CD)
  carries details about more than
  25,000 courses.*

- National Extension College
  18 Brooklands Avenue,
  Cambridge CB2 2HN
  (Tel: 0223-316644)
  *Offers a range of courses
  including GCSE subjects,
  preparatory courses for Open
  University, office skills, and
  personal development.*

- National Open Learning
    Library
  BOLDU Ltd
  St George's House
  40–49 Price Street
  Birmingham B4 6LA
  (Tel: 021-359-6628)
  *Has 6000 items for
  inspection by visitors
  —but no borrowing.*

- Open College
  St Pauls
  781 Wilmslow Road
  Didsbury
  Manchester M20 8RW
  (Tel: 061-434-0007)
  *Offers a range of materials
  in such areas as accountancy,
  management, information
  technology and retailing.*

- Open College of the Arts
  Worsburgh
  Barnsley
  South Yorkshire
  S70 6TU
  (Tel: 0226-730495)
  *Practical courses on art and design,
  painting, sculpture, textiles,
  photography and creative writing.*

- *Open Learning Directory*
  Published annually by
  Pergamon Press, Oxford
  *Details of 2000-plus packages in
  professional and vocational training.*

- Open Learning Foundation
  24 Angel Gate
  City Road
  London
  EC1V 2RS
  (Tel: 071-833-3757)
  *Widening range of undergraduate
  course materials being put together
  by consortiumof the former
  polytechnics.*

- Open University and
  Open Business School
  Milton Keynes
  MK7 6AA
  (Tel: 0908-274066)
  *Many other organizations
  now run courses based on OU
  materials in undergraduate
  education and in vocational and
  professional updating courses
  —e.g. in management, health
  service and social work, teaching,
  and technology.*

How about doing a "wrap around"?

You may find that no suitable open learning materials have yet been published. Or if they have, you can't afford to use them or adapt them.

So must you then give up the idea of using open learning? Or else embark on the possibly long and costly task of developing your own materials from scratch? Perhaps neither. There may be a middle way . . .

*Although you have not been able to find suitable open learning material, you may be able to find **other** usable material. That is, you may know of books, videos, audiotapes, etc that—while **not** produced with open learning (or maybe any sort of learning) in mind—still do a pretty good job of getting your subject matter across.*

e.g. consider:

~ textbooks
~ manuals
~ pamphlets
~ newspaper clippings
~ journal articles
~ commercial leaflets
~ government pamphlets
~ videos/photographs
~ audiotapes/discs
~ practical kits
~ CBT packs

If so, you may consider writing a study guide that "wraps around" the chosen item or items and makes up for whatever they lack in open learning terms. (See opposite for some suggestions.)

"Wrap-arounds"

You may sometimes be able to build your package around existing material—e.g. a textbook, a set of pamphlets or a series of videos. In this case you may need to customize it with a workbook or study guide containing, e.g.:

- Advice on how to use the material

- Learning objectives

- Introductions/overviews

- Summaries

- Glossaries

- Clearer explanations

- Contrasting viewpoints

- Alternative examples

- Illustrations

- Local case studies

- Activities (especially locally relevant ones)

- Feedback on such activities

- Instructions for practical work

- Assignments for discussion with tutor, mentor, line manager, colleagues, etc.

o *Other possible items? (What?)*

You may also want to add new media—e.g. audiotapes.

Checklist—evaluating existing materials

AUDIENCE

For whom is it intended—e.g. what prior knowledge, interest, experience, attitudes and learning skills does it assume? Is its target audience sufficiently like ours?

OBJECTIVES

Does it have learning objectives sufficiently similar to those of our learners?

ASSESSMENT

How is assessment catered for (if at all) within the materials? Is this consistent with what we might want for our learners?

COVERAGE

Is the subject-matter appropriate to our learners and the objectives? Is it accurate and up to date? Broad enough? Balanced? Any serious omissions?

TIME

How much time might the materials (including any assessment) demand of learners? Is this realistic for our learners?

TEACHING

Is the teaching method (e.g. didactic v experiential) acceptable? Are media used appropriately? What kind of demands might be made on support staff—e.g. advisers, tutors, line managers, mentors, etc? Can we provide the necessary individual support?

STYLE

Is the style of the material suitable for our learners —e.g. tone, vocabulary, sentence length, examples, use of pictorial material? Is it lively and interesting?

PHYSICAL FORMAT

Is it attractive in appearance? Legible? Durable? Portable? Suited to how it will be used?

REPUTATION

Does the material (and/or the producers) have a "track record"? Who has used it before? How well has it been received by other users?

COSTS

How much to hire or buy? What additional costs are there—e.g. video players, support system, training time, adaptations to materials? Is this within our budget and/or that of our learners?

AVAILABILITY

How easily/quickly can we obtain sufficient copies? Will it continue to be available?

LIKELY BENEFITS

Are learners likely to get what they would expect from using the materials? Is the organization?

ALTERNATIVES

How does this material compare with other existing material and with what we might produce ourselves?

Development activities

1   If you'd like more ideas about adapting existing material, read:

- *LEWIS & PAINE (1986) (pages 9–63)*
- *KEMBER (1991).*

    Then:

2   Consult colleagues, catalogues and databases to see what material exists in your subject-area.

3   Obtain inspection copies of likely-sounding materials.

4   Evaluate the material, preferably with the help of colleagues—and maybe learners. (The checklist opposite may be useful in this.)

5   Make a list of what you would need to provide in addition to existing open learning materials—or of the contents of your study guide in the case of a 'wrap around'.

6   Weigh up the costs—in time, money and effort—of using existing materials versus making your own. Decide accordingly.

Even if you decide not to use any of the existing materials, you may still find that you pick up a lot of ideas you can use in making your own.

Copyright warning

Remember—if you decide to have your learners work with existing materials, you must respect copyright law. (See also page 148.)

For instance, you can't freely reprint newspaper cuttings and journal articles. Nor can you make your own compilation of titbits from texts and manuals you just happen to like the look of.

EITHER you or the learners must pay for copies of any items you use

OR   you must negotiate with the owners of the copyright to let you reproduce their material in your own form.

Stage 2

Preparing for writing

Route map for materials preparation

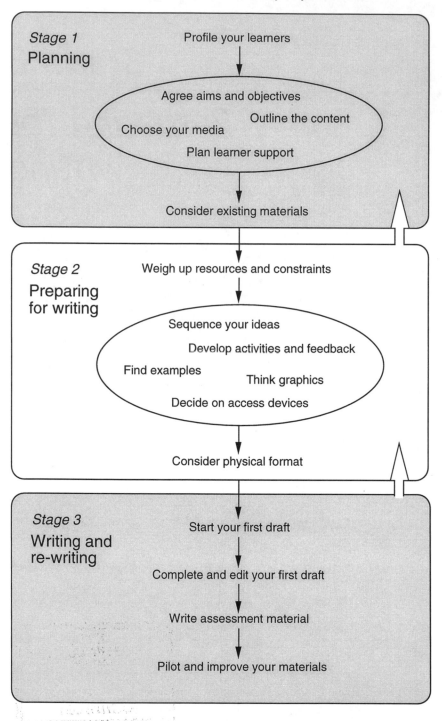

Task 2a

Weigh up your resources and constraints

Before launching into developing your materials, it's worth pausing to get a few things clear in your mind:

- Who is expecting what of you?

- What resources can you call on in your project?

- How will you schedule your time?

Identifying expectations

Are you developing materials purely for your own satisfaction? Or are you writing them partly to satisfy your boss, a client, a course team, or any other "interested parties"? If so, now's the time to ask them what it is they're expecting —before you begin.

Counting your resources

You can't develop materials out of nothing. You'll need resources. The chief of these will be your own time, skill and energy. But you may also need help from other people. And you may need the use of equipment and facilities—and perhaps even some hard cash.

Be as realistic as possible about what resources are available to you. If you are over-optimistic you may agree to develop a more ambitious set of materials than is humanly possible.

Planning your time

How are you to spend your time? Colleagues may be able to give you a rough idea of the total amount you'll need. (And it's always a fair bet you'll need 50 per cent more than you expect.) Estimates commonly vary between 10 and 100 hours of development time for every hour of learning time. One cannot be more precise without knowing more about the nature of the project and the skills of the developers.

But how will you spread your time over the days or weeks ahead? This will depend in part on how much time you expect to spend on each stage and each task.

You may find it useful to rough out a time allocation as I have done on the opposite page. Once I get into my project, things may turn out differently than I expect. But, at present, you'll see that I am expecting to spend half my time on Stages 1 and 2, and the other half on Stage 3. Within each stage, my timings are even more notional, but you'll see that I am expecting to spend 10 or 20 times as much on some tasks as on others. You may want to allocate your time quite differently—as I might on another project.

Scheduling your work

If you are working to a deadline—or if your work must tie with other people's—you'll also need a schedule. Your schedule should show your key dates. For instance:

• When will you be expecting to consult certain colleagues?

• When do you want some learners available to try out your materials?

• By when will you need multiple copies of the material?

How much time per task?

A = My estimate of how **I** might share out the time I have available for a certain materials project.

B = Your estimate of how you might expect to share out **your** time.

C = The times you actually spend on each task—which you may like to fill in as you go along, as a guide for when you next come to write materials. (Watch out for those extra few minutes you spend here and there on a task, perhaps days after you made your main effort on it.)

	A %	B %	C %
Stage 1—Planning your materials	25		
1a Profile your learners	3		
1b Agree aims and objectives	8		
1c Outline the content	8		
1d Choose your media	2		
1e Plan for learner support	1		
1f Consider existing materials	3		
Stage 2—Preparing for writing	25		
2a Weigh up your resources and constraints	2		
2b Sequence your ideas	3		
2c Develop activities and feedback	10		
2d Find examples	6		
2e Think graphics	2		
2f Decide on access devices	1		
2g Consider the physical format	1		
Stage 3—Writing and re-writing	50		
3a Start your first draft	15		
3b Complete and edit your first draft	10		
3c Write assessment material	5		
3d Pilot and improve your materials	20		

Development activities

1 If you'd like some more ideas
   about what is involved in getting
   organized for materials
   development, read:

   • TTSI (pages 19–33)

              Then:

2 Draw up a schedule with the help
   of experienced colleagues (if you
   have any)—or get their comments
   on any schedule you have already
   been presented with.

3 Make a note of your answers to
   the questions in the checklists pn
   pages 91 and 92—and of any
   other such questions that occur
   to you.

4 Check your ideas by discussing
   them with colleagues if possible.

5 Revise your plans as necessary in
   the light of the feedback you get.

Expectations checklist

- Who needs to be satisfied with your materials besides yourself—e.g. colleagues, "clients", your boss, your learners, your learners' bosses, etc?

- What possibly different expectations might those people have? How can you find out?

- How might you resolve any conflict between their different expectations?

- By what criteria will the overall success of your materials development be judged? And by whom?

- Will you have full responsibility for developing the materials or will you work as one of a "course team"?

- How free will you be to make the final decisions about the content, approach and physical format of the materials?

Resources checklist

- How much time can you make available for developing your materials?

- How much help (and therefore time) might you need from colleagues—e.g. word processor operators, editors, designers, subject experts, learners, etc.?

- If you need expert help that you can't get within your organization, to what extent might you be able to buy it in from outside?

- How much cash can you spend on developing your materials?

- Will you be able to provide any support or facilities that will be needed by learners who are working on your materials—e.g. audio-visual hardware, library facilities, access to support staff, a room to meet in?

- Are you satisfied that you have sufficient resources to do a satisfactory job? If not, what might you do about it?

- How confident are you about your own competence for the project? How might you obtain additional training if you feel it might be helpful?

Scheduling checklist

- Have you scheduled for all the crucial **deadlines** you must meet—e.g. the availability of colleagues or clients before they go on holiday, the dates of important meetings, the date when learners need to start working through your materials?

- Does your schedule allow you at least as much time for planning and preparing as you have for writing?

- Have you agreed the target dates with other "interested parties"—e.g. your boss, clients, colleagues? Under what conditions, and to what extent, might they be happy about your amending the dates later, if need be?

- Does your schedule take account of holidays and other predictable interruptions?

- Have you booked any equipment, staff or facilities you will need to use?

- Can you see how you might, if necessary, make more time for your materials—e.g. by slowing down some other activity or by getting additional help?

NOTE: *If this is your first attempt at materials development, you may be unsure as to how long the various tasks will take you. (You should find it easier next time, when you've had some experience.) Be prepared to* **adjust** *this first schedule once you know how long things are taking.*

o In answering the above questions you may have identified some CONSTRAINTS—factors that might prevent you producing the package you'd ideally like to produce.

o If so, what might you do to lessen or remove these constraints?

Task 2b

Sequence your ideas

As a result of your work on Task 1c, you should have a good idea of the topics that must be covered in your materials. Are you writing only a couple of hours' worth of learning material? If so, your topics may be few in number.

But perhaps you're planning to keep learners occupied for several days? In that case, you may have a much longer list.

Either way, most of us need **more** than a list of topics before we start writing. We may first need to decide:

- What are the chief teaching points we want to make about each topic.
- In what order we are going to tackle them.
- What will be the overall structure of our materials.

How will you set about sequencing **your** ideas? On the next page, I list some approaches I have often found useful.

Some useful approaches

Here are five approaches I have often found useful when sequencing my ideas for learning materials:

- **Drawing diagrams** (illustrated on pages 60 and 61).

- **Analysing my objectives.** (Pages 54 and 97 show how teasing out the sub-objectives from a main objective can suggest sub-topics and help us think about possible sequences.)

- **Thinking about activities** (the subject of Task 2c).

- **Listing my teaching points.** (See page 98.)

- **Keeping an open mind.** The ideal structure for my materials sometimes dawns on me out of nowhere it seems—perhaps while washing up or driving to work. I suddenly "see" how, for instance, the whole thing might be organized around a series of tasks that learners can carry out in any order they choose or around a tape-recording of the discussion I had with learners about the topic in a workshop situation. But such "visions" still need a lot of work doing on them!

Which sequence are we talking about?

- The sequence in which you learned the subject?

  Which may not be the one your learners would find most helpful.

- The sequence in which you've taught it in the past?

  Which may not be ideal for learners learning on their own.

- The subject's traditional or "natural" sequence?

  Which may be a helpful way for "experts" to picture the subject but not for novices.

- The sequence which you think up for it?

  Which may differ from any mentioned above.

- The sequence in which you write it?

  And you don't have to write it in the sequence in which you will present it or expect learners to work on it.

- The sequence in which you present it?

  You may or may not be expecting learners to work on units in the order in which they are presented—e.g. as chapters in a book.

- The sequence your learner chooses to follow?

  And different learners may choose quite different sequences through your material.

Remember—what seems like the most obvious sequence to you and your fellow-experts may not seem so to all of your learners.

Types of sequence

*You might want to use one of these
for the programme as a whole and
one or more of the others for sections within it*

- **Random topics**   When it wouldn't matter in which order learners tackled your topics. One doesn't necessarily depend on another.

- **Chronological**   Where it makes sense to discuss topics in the order in which they happen over time.

- **Place-to-place**   Where you start by talking about one place and then move on to discuss adjacent places, e.g. sections in a store.

- **Concentric circles**   Where each topic or idea you talk about includes all the previous topics you've talked about.

- **Causal sequence**   Following a chain of cause-and-effect from first cause to final effect.

- **Structural logic**   Where certain ideas or skills must be tackled earlier in order for later ones to make sense.

- **Problem-centred**   Where your sequence arises out of getting learners to explore some central problem or case.

- **Spiral sequence**   In which you keep revisiting ideas looked at earlier, but in greater depth each time.

- **Backward chaining**   Where you have a chain of tasks and it makes sense to teach the last one first, then the second to last, and so on.

Breaking down your objectives

—e.g. from course aims and objectives
—to unit objectives
—to section objectives

Course aim: To introduce students to the basics of historical research and communication.

Course objective: Students will learn how to carry out historical research projects and present their findings in an appropriate form.

Unit objective 1:   The student will be able to make efficient and critical use of all the sources available.

Section objectives—The student will be able to:

(a)   Distinguish between primary and secondary sources.

(b)   Identify primary sources appropriate to the various kinds of historical data he or she requires.

(c)   Assess the likely bias and credibility of a secondary source.

(d)   Determine the usefulness of a source.

(e)   Suggest ways of finding suitable sources.

(f)   Distinguish between valid and invalid inferences that might be made from a source.

Unit objective 2—   The student will be able to communicate his or her findings clearly and concisely in writing, using an approach appropriate to the readers being aimed at.

Section objectives—The student will be able to:

(What section objectives might Unit objective 2 suggest?)

See also page 54 for another example of objectives teased out into sub-objectives.

From topics to teaching points

You may sometimes find it useful to expand your list of topics (headings) into a list of **teaching points**—*the statements you want to make about each topic. For example:*

SUBJECT: "Costing an open learning scheme"

TOPICS: A. The need for costing
             B. Open v conventional costs
             C. Estimating your costs
             D. Comparing costs . . . *AND SO ON*

TEACHING POINTS:

A1   Costing can help you and your learners in a number of ways . . .

A2   Open learning schemes need to be accurately costed.

A3   The danger of under-costing is . . .

A4   The danger of over-costing is . . . *AND SO ON*

B1   Open learning (OL) is not necessarily less costly than conventional learning (CL).

B2   But it may still be more cost-effective.

B3   The chief cost factor is the time of staff and learners.

B4   The economics of OL depends on the balance between fixed and variable costs.

B5   Fixed costs are . . .

B6   Variable costs are . . .

B7   Fixed and variable costs differ between OL and CL because . . .

B8   We need to find the "break-even point" . . . *AND SO ON*

C1   Your focus in costing will differ according to whether you are a producer, deliverer, sponsor or learner.

C2   The chief production costs are as follows . . .

C3   The chief delivery and support costs are as follows . . . *AND SO ON*

Each teaching point may become the basis for one or more paragraphs of your material.

Development activities

1   If you'd like more ideas about sequencing your ideas, read:

- TTSI
  (pages 61–71 and 137–51)

- LAURILLARD (1993)
  (chapter 10)

- DCfS (pages 72–132).

Then:

2   Break down your topics and try to draft an outline of the key points you need to make. (You may prefer to work on this with a colleague.)

3   Get comments on your draft outline from one or more colleagues.

4   Revise your outline as seems necessary in the light of the feedback you get.

Checklist

- Has this task given you any ideas for changes in the list of content you produced in Task 1c?

- Has it given you any ideas for changes in objectives?

- Have you thought of any points that might be best taught by some media other than those you originally had in mind?

- Do you feel you have sorted out all the teaching points necessary to cover the content you outlined in Task 1c?

- Do these teaching points do justice to the key concepts in your subject?

- Are any of your "points" still really topics (headings) that need breaking down yet further—into the points (statements) that need making about those topics?

- How confident are you that you begin and end with the most appropriate points and that the sequence of points in between is a reasonable one? (Remembering, of course, that there may be many different justifiable sequences.)

- Is it clear how each of your points links to those before and after it?

- Have you missed out any important linking points?

- Have you included points that introduce new sections, give overviews or sum up on what has gone before?

- Have you thought about whether to advise all learners to follow the same route through your materials or to encourage them (and enable them) to choose their own individual sequences?

Where possible, write your materials in such a way as to allow learners some choice about the sequence in which they work through them.

Task 2c

Develop activities and feedback

Open learning is meant to be active learning. Our learners are usually expected to **do something** with the ideas they are learning about.

They can then be given "feedback"—or obtain it for themselves. This should help them confirm their understanding or else improve it.

Activity plus feedback plays a vital role in helping the learner to learn.

Types of activity

This learner activity may be prompted in several ways—e.g.:

- Questions or exercises embedded in the material—every few minutes perhaps—inviting the learner to answer a question or carry out some practical work before continuing that section.

- Sets of questions (self-tests) at the end of a section—e.g, several pages or screens of reading—which test what the learner has gained from the section as a whole.

- Assignments or exercises (often for assessment by a tutor) that are to be tackled after perhaps many hours of work—sometimes involving extensive practical or project work.

In Task 2c you will be chiefly concerned with the first type listed above. These are often labelled "activities", "exercises" or "self-assessment questions" (SAQs). The other two types we'll need to think more about in Task 3c.

The displays on the following pages should help you sort out some activities on your own topic.

Activities—why have them?

*Writers of open learning materials say that
activities can help learners to:*

- Remember the ideas in the package.

- Understand the ideas in the package.

- Make use of the ideas in the package.

- Think for themselves.

- Learn by doing.

- Go beyond memorization.

- Relate the teaching to their own situation.

- Bring in their own experience and examples.

- Reflect on their own thoughts and feelings.

- Obtain information that the package cannot provide.

- Apply their learning to their work or personal life.

- Practise towards important objectives.

- Monitor their own progress.

- Identify their strengths and weaknesses.

- Keep a record of what they have done.

o *Might you have any other purposes? (What?)*

*Which of the above purposes might seem
most important to your LEARNERS?*

What might learners DO?

Activities may make a wide range of demands on learners. They might, for example, be asked to:

- Recall content.

- Restate content in their own words.

- Apply their new learning to given examples.

- Suggest their own examples.

- Compare or evaluate new ideas.

- Reflect on how their own experience relates.

- Take on different roles.

- Practise what they have learned.

- Examine new materials in the light of what they have learned so far.

- Interview or discuss with other people.

- Carry out practical work.

o *Any others that occur to you? (What?)*

How might learners make their response?

With different sorts of activity, learners might be expected to make their response in a variety of different forms. Learners might be asked to:

- Just think their response (no record).

- Tick boxes in a checklist.

- Press keys on a computer keyboard.

- Answer a multiple-choice question.

- Underline phrases in a text.

- Complete a table.

- Fill in blanks left in a sentence.

- Write a word/phrase/number in a box or in the margin.

- Write or key in a sentence or paragraph.

- Write out the steps in a calculation.

- Add to a graph, chart, diagram, etc.

- Draw a graph, chart, diagram, etc.

- Make a tape recording.

- Take photographs.

o *Any others that occur to you? (What?)*

In general, the simpler the form of response required, the more likely learners are to tackle the activity

Helping learners get benefit from activities

Despite our best intentions, learners don't usually tackle all our activities. So how can we make it more likely they'll at least tackle those that will most benefit them? Here are some suggestions:

- Have key activity responses assessed by tutor.

- Use activity responses as basis for group work.

- Ensure activity is clearly relevant to learner's work/life.

- Make clear how each activity contributes to an objective.

- Tell learner the purpose of activities
  ~ in general
  ~ in individual cases.

- Indicate time needed for an activity.

- Suggest how big an answer is appropriate.

- Avoid "busy-work" (trivial and Mickey Mouse exercises).

- Avoid vague activities (e.g. "Jot down a few ideas about...").

- Avoid non-essential writing (consider tick boxes) or keying.

- Ensure variety.

- Use typography or graphic signals to emphasize activities.

- Provide for satisfying **feedback**, e.g.
  ~ correct answers if there are any
  ~ sample answers if many would be correct
  ~ the results of a choice they have made
  ~ other people's responses (e.g. from pilot learners)
  ~ advice as to how they can assess their own responses
  ~ advice about how to get feedback from other people
  ~ sympathy about difficulties they may have had
  ~ reassurance about possible errors they may have made
  ~ comments on issues raised by the activities.

Two contrasting activities
In extracts from two different courses for managers

1—the "tutorial-in-print" approach (see page 14)

Here, for instance, is a sales manager talking about the kinds of problems he is experiencing:

> "We're getting really behind on deliveries. The production guys just don't seem to appreciate that the buyers for this new steel are much more demanding than the customers who buy our other products. And we've got technical problems because the production department is basically handling the new steel in just the same way as the other metals—and this isn't good enough for a high-specification product like this. We're soon going to be out-flanked by our competitors. I'm pushing for some pretty basic re-organization around here, I can tell you"

Activity Q: What kind of hierarchy (Functional or Product) would you say this man is working in? What kind of re-organization might he be hoping for?

✴✴✴✴✴✴✴✴✴✴✴✴✴✴✴✴✴✴✴✴✴✴✴✴✴✴✴✴✴✴✴✴✴✴✴✴✴✴✴

In fact, he was in a company producing speciality ferrous metals that had recently diversified into producing a new steel for the aircraft industry. It was organized on functional lines. Although it had set up a new sales department to deal with the new product and its new type of customers, production was left to the existing department which was also responsible for the wider range of products. The sales manager hoped for, and eventually got, a separate production facility to concentrate on the new steel with all its quite new demands.

2—the "reflective action guide" approach (see page 15)

Drafting an advertisement

Now draft an advertisement for one of the posts you considered in Sections 2 and 3. Refer to the job description and person specification you drafted in those sections.

Get comments on your draft from a colleague in Personnel and/or from someone else with experience of recruiting the kind of staff you are looking for. (You may also want to get comments from someone doing the kind of job you are advertising.)

Improve your advert in the light of these comments.

Draft advertisements for any further posts you need to fill.

N.B. Does anyone need to approve your advertisements? If so, consider at what stage you might want to show them your drafts.

> *Drafting effective job advertisements is never a routine task. Can you be sure you have said just what is necessary to encourage the suitable and discourage the others? And does your advertisement present the appropriate public image of your organization? No matter how experienced you get, it is always worth asking a colleague for a second opinion on your drafts.*

Development activities

1 If you'd like more ideas about using activities, read:

- EXPLODL
  (pages 128–32; 134–7)

- TTSI (pages 119–135)

- LOCKWOOD (1992).

You may want to follow this reading by seeing how activities have been used in whatever range of open learning materials you can lay your hands on.

Then:

2 Select some of your objectives or sub-objectives and draft activities that should help learners in attaining them.

3 Consider what kind of feedback might be appropriate and draft suitable comments to follow each activity.

4 Get some colleagues—and some learners if possible—to comment on your drafts.

5 Decide which of your draft activities and feedback are still worth including in your materials and improve them in the light of the comments you have had.

Checklist

- Is the purpose of each activity clear to you? Will it be clear to learners?

- Can you say how each activity helps towards a particular objective? If not, why is it worth tackling?

- Will learners be clear about how big an answer you expect, or how long to spend on it?

- What have you done to make it more likely that learners will tackle the activity?

- How reasonable is it that learners should be able to make a fair crack at the activity at this stage of their learning? Will they have the necessary experience, information or skill?

- What will you suggest learners do if they find difficulty with the activity?

- Have you allowed for sufficient variety—e.g. types of exercise, ways of responding—among your activities?

- In terms of the list given in the final item on page 105, how satisfied are learners likely to be with the feedback?

- Where will you display your feedback or comments—e.g. directly after the activity or elsewhere? Why?

- Have you produced both activities you already know the right answers to and activities where different learners may produce different right answers (which you cannot predict)? If your activities are all of one type, try writing some of the other.

- If you are trying to develop learners' competence at work, do any of your activities help them relate their learning to their workplace? If not, try writing such an activity.

- Have you thought of any ways in which learners' friends or colleagues might be able to give them feedback?

> If you've not yet thought about examples (Task 2d) and graphics (Task 2e), you may find that doing so gives you yet more ideas about suitable activities.

Task 2d
Find examples

Imagine how this book would seem if I'd shown you no "for instances". No examples of open learning materials. No examples of objectives or activities. Not even examples of examples!

Very dry, that's how. Abstract. Vague. Difficult to relate to your own concerns. You might literally not have known what I was talking about.

The best teachers have always known that people can have difficulty with abstract ideas. They need examples. For instance: Jesus was well aware of our need for examples. He knew better than to lecture on ethical and theological principles. Instead he told stories about people like his listeners. It was those examples that brought the ideas to life.

For me, working up a set of really telling examples is often one of the most challenging and surprisingly time-consuming tasks in a writing project.

The following pages may help you think about why **your** learners might need examples—and how to find the most appropriate ones.

Bringing your ideas to life

Your open learning materials are likely to be full of new ideas, new theories and new methods—new to the learner, that is. They will all be capable of altering the ways your learners see the world and the ways they act upon it.

But your new ideas will get across to learners only if:

- you teach through examples;
- the examples mean something to your learners;
- your learners are encouraged to provide examples of their own; and
- you get learners to work with the examples—e.g. through activities.

If you've already tackled Task 2c (activities), you may have thought up some examples already. The displays on the next few pages may help you take your thinking further.

Examples may take many forms, e.g.:

- References to things learners already know—like my parables of Jesus example on page 109.
- Analogies that bring out similarities between what learners already know and what they are learning about.
- Anecdotes—that illustrate the idea being discussed.
- Human interest stories.
- Cameos of people in relevant situations. (See Item 1 on page 106.)
- Case studies and simulations the learner can explore.
- Pictures—drawings, photographs, diagrams, maps, etc.
- Jokes or cartoons—if they really do bring out a principle or make it memorable.
- Audio and video material—e.g. recordings of interviews or of work in factories, laboratories, hospitals, etc.
- Real objects—e.g. rock specimens or fabric swatches.
- Graphs or charts and tables of figures.
- Calculations showing all the steps to a solution.
- Quotations from other subject experts.
- Comments from "interested parties"—customers, clients, patients, parents, children, etc.
- Examples provided by earlier learners—e.g. of workplace experiences or other life events and relationships.
- Examples that current learners are asked to provide from their own experience, probably in response to an activity. (See Item 2 on page 106.)
- Visits to farms and factories, museums and galleries, shops and offices, geological sites, and so on.
- *Others you might use? (What?)*

How many of these types can you find among the examples on pages 113 and 114?

How to find examples

- Reflect on your own experience.

- Adapt examples (and activities?) that have worked well in your face-to-face teaching.

- Read widely—books, journals, newspapers, etc.

- View video material.

- Ask a colleague.

- Brainstorm with a group of colleagues.

- Ask your clients (if you have any) or your learners' sponsors.

- Interview other people with experience of your subject —both providers (e.g. doctors) and "customers" (e.g. patients).

- Develop a network of people who will be happy to have you ring up and ask for a comment or example from their experience.

- Get people of the kind who might become your learners to tell you about their experience of the subject and how they see it.

- Be alert for examples that occur to you out of the blue while doing the washing up or walking the dog.

- Write activities that get your learners to relate the ideas being discussed to their own experience.

- Ask learners to find examples of their own to work on.

o *Others? (What?)*

Examples of verbal examples

A bar of toffee warmed in the hand will bend easily, but is difficult to break. If you cool it in a refrigerator, it will break easily. Even warm toffee can be br⟨

back of a spoon

The force in the bar is $1500\,\text{N}$.
The area of the bar is
$$5\,\text{mm} \times 5\,\text{mm} = 25\,\text{mm}^2$$
$$\text{Stress} = \frac{\text{force}}{\text{area}}$$
So stress in the bar is given by
$$\text{stress} = \frac{1500\,\text{N}}{25\,\text{mm}^2} = 60\,\text{N}\,\text{mm}^{-2}$$

Here are some examples of activities which pilot students on the course identified as showing the use of communication skills:

" *The last job interview I did I had to find out what sor organisation it was, what sort of skills they were looking and present my own case in writing through the applic tion, and verbally at the interview, to match this.* "

" *A report I had to produce last yea*

SAQ 1

Are the following failures of a st⟨ to lack of strength or lack of stif

A   A chair breaks when you sit

B   A chair sags too much wher

C   When loaded, the bottom o the ground on a hump-back

D   A car tyre bursts

Video Case Study
This case study concern office procedures. It wil to apply what you have, to take the role of a new tasked with introducing ⟨ handling conflict.

The scenario will raise a number of key questions which you⟨ a manager w⟨

Patient 1

Doctor   'Hello Mrs Smith, I haven't seen you for ages, come and sit d⟨

Patient 1 'I
ε

Doctor
Patient 1

of the residents' social club. The
the local paper shows how initiatives taken by a governor
and headteacher established a tradition at the school.

FORDBRIDGE SCHOOL – *Senior Citizens' Party*

Christmas came on 3rd December to the Fordbridge School
when pupils played host to the Senior Citizens of the area. To
call it a tea-party would be an understatement, as about 350
guests crowded into the festively decorated sch⟨
A Victorian-style 'Good Old D⟨
the proceedings with a⟨
girls' ch⟨
shop q⟨
course ⟨
songs.
Tea ha⟨
helpers wh⟨
went home⟨
in bud. pl⟨

I took the epigraph ⟨
longer version of whicl
fear that the creative ⟨
something of its philoso

Finally, a brief exampl⟨

Tyger! Tyger! burni⟨
In the fore⟨
Wh⟨
Cou⟨

Mrs P lives in a Victorian terrace in an inner-city area. She left school early, but is bright and receptive to new ideas. She is a warm, welcoming, mature person who loves children but is not possessive. She reads widely, and has developed a keen interest i⟨ child development.
Mrs P started ⟨
friend. Her⟨
up ⟨

If, for example, I collect masses of facts about which political party people voted for at the last election I am merely producing a description of what happened. But ⟨begin to make certain connections between these ⟨come as more significant than others ⟨with them, beginning to use ⟨as about how to ⟨ions

Choose a teenage boy or girl well known to you. (They can be your own son or daughter, the child of a relative or friend, or a young person where you work.) W⟨⟨ down all the things that *puzzle* you about this person's behavio⟨   ⟨you perceive them.

Let us take some more examples of case (1). How about this?

All philosophers are millionaires
I am a philosopher

Therefore: I am a millionaire.

produce heat. Many of these reactions will be familiar to you, e.g.

$$\text{glucose} + 6\text{O}_2 \longrightarrow 6\text{CO}_2 + 6\text{H}_2\text{O}; \Delta G^{\ominus\prime} = -2\,870\,\text{kJ}\,\text{mol}^{-1} \quad (2.8)$$

$$\text{glucose} \longrightarrow 2\,\text{lactate}; \Delta G^{\ominus\prime} = -192\,\text{kJ}\,\text{mol}^{-1} \quad (2.9)$$

$$\text{palmitate} + 23\text{O}_2 \longrightarrow 16\text{CO}_2 + 16\text{H}_2\text{O}; \Delta G^{\ominus\prime} = -9\,782\,\text{kJ}\,\text{mol}^{-1} \quad (2.10)$$

$$\text{lactate} + 3\text{O}_2 \longrightarrow 3\text{CO}_2 + 3\text{H}_2\text{O}; \Delta G^{\ominus\prime} = -1\,339\,\text{kJ}\,\text{mol}^{-1} \quad (2.11)$$

Examples of graphic examples

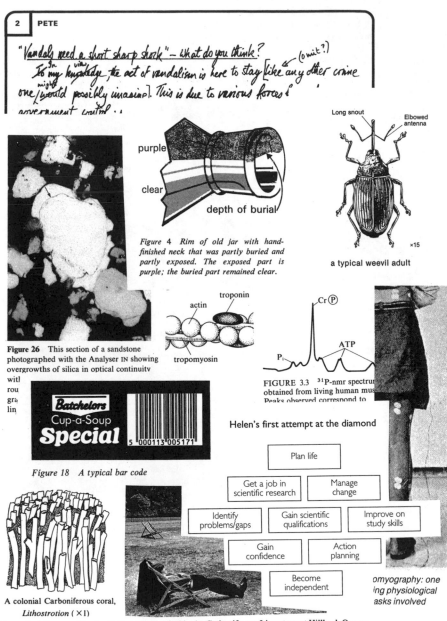

2   PETE

"Vandals need a short sharp shock" – what do you think?
To my knowledge, the act of vandalism is here to stay [like any other crime (omit?)
one/would possibly imagine]. This is due to various forces of
government control . .

purple

clear

depth of burial

Figure 4   Rim of old jar with hand-
finished neck that was partly buried and
partly exposed. The exposed part is
purple; the buried part remained clear.

Long snout

Elbowed
antenna

×15

a typical weevil adult

Figure 26   This section of a sandstone
photographed with the Analyser IN showing
overgrowths of silica in optical continuity
with
rou
gra
lin

troponin

actin

tropomyosin

Cr P

ATP

P_i

FIGURE 3.3 ^{31}P-nmr spectrum
obtained from living human mus
Peaks observed correspond to

Batchelors
Cup-a-Soup
Special

5 000113 005171

Figure 18   A typical bar code

Helen's first attempt at the diamond

Plan life

Get a job in
scientific research

Manage
change

Identify
problems/gaps

Gain scientific
qualifications

Improve on
study skills

Gain
confidence

Action
planning

Become
independent

omyography: one
ing physiological
asks involved

A colonial Carboniferous coral,
   Lithostrotion (×1)

Examples of some of the fossils that you may find in the Carboniferous Limestone at Hillbeck Quarry.

Development activities

1 *For more ideas about the use of examples (and other teaching techniques), read:*

   - *TTSI (pages 137–61)*

2 *If you want to see more examples of examples, read:*

   - *TTSI (pages 92–117).*

   - *EXPLODL (pages 155–74)*

   - *pages 18–38 in this book*

   and look through any other open learning materials you can find.

   Then:

3 *Work up a few examples that you might use in your materials and write yourself a memo about how you would use each one and what purpose it would serve.*
   (Note: Even if you are preparing a 'wrap-around' you may still need examples in addition to those in the core text.)

4 *Discuss your examples with colleagues and, if possible, with learners. Get their reactions not just to the examples but also to how you plan to use them.*

5 *Revise your ideas as necessary in the light of the feedback you get.*

Checklist

- Have you been able to think of examples for all the main ideas you'll be dealing with? If not, how might you use the suggestions on page 112 to find more?

- Have you been able to get ideas for examples from people like your future learners?

- If you are writing for someone else's learners, have you looked for ideas from your clients?

- How sure are you that learners will find your examples understandable and relevant—especially if they vary greatly in their backgrounds or needs?

- Are your examples sufficiently clear-cut—without complications that learners are not yet prepared for?

- If you are working at a more advanced level, are your examples (especially case studies) rich enough to allow for a sufficiently wide variety of responses?

- Have you seen ways of helping learners bring their own examples into play—e.g. through activities, assignments or workplace projects?

- Do your examples include "human interest" (that is, tell stories about people) where appropriate?

- Might any of your examples be made more effective by basing activities on them (See Task 2c)?

- Have you considered how your available media might effectively present different kinds of example—e.g. print, audio, video, CBT, etc?

> *You may find it worth keeping a notebook (and maybe a box file for graphic and audio-visual examples) to record ideas that occur to you out of the blue and that might otherwise get forgotten.*

Task 2e

Think graphics

What are we talking about here? Simply any way of presenting information in print that is **not** a solid block of prose. Solid prose can daunt even the keenest learner—especially if it covers page after page. A graphic approach can both cheer the reader and help get your message across.

Graphs, drawings, photographs and other pictures would be obvious examples of graphics. But if you turned prose into **lists** or **tables** you would also be taking a graphic approach.

Alongside is a slightly more graphic way of saying what I have said above:

Ideas can be presented in two different ways:

1. As solid prose. (But too much can daunt even keen learners.)

2. Graphically (which may be clearer and more cheering), e.g. by using:

   • prose in lists, tables, etc, or

   • pictures (graphs, drawings, photographs,etc).

And here is an even more graphic version:

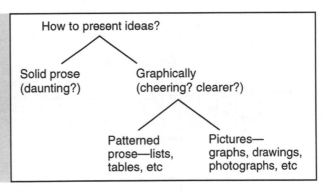

How to present ideas?

Solid prose (daunting?)

Graphically (cheering? clearer?)

Patterned prose—lists, tables, etc

Pictures— graphs, drawings, photographs, etc

Page 118 shows another example of prose being made graphic.

As for pictures, page 119 suggests reasons for using them.

Making prose more graphic

*Material presented first as solid prose (version A)
—then made increasingly graphic (versions B, C and D).*

A

If your soil specimen feels gritty, like sand, and is
sticky, then if you can polish it between your
fingers, it is a **sandy clay loam**. If it does not
polish, then it is a **sandy silt loam**. If it is gritt
but NOT sticky, and you can mould it into a b
that holds together, it is a **sandy loam**. If you
can't mould it into such a ball, then it is a **sand**
Furthermore, if it leaves a mark when you rut
on a patch of clean skin, it is a **loamy sand**. If
soil is NOT gritty but feels silky (creamy) and
can polish it and change its shape, it is a **silty**
loam. If you can't change its shape it is a **clay**
the soil feels gritty and silky, but won't polish
a **silt loam** (if clearly silky) or a **silty loam**. If i
neither gritty nor silky, then it is just a **loam**.

B

1. Soil feels **gritty** (like sand)   ...Go to 2
   Soil does **not** feel gritty   ...Go to 4

2. Soil feels **sticky**   ...Go to 3
   Soil does **not** feel sticky   ...Go to 9

3. Soil will **polish** when rubbed
                    between fingers   ...**Sandy clay loam**
   Soil will **not** polish   ...**Sandy silt loam**

4. Soil feels **silky** (creamy)   ...Go to 5
   Soil does **not** feel silky   ...**Loam**

5. Soil will **polish** when rubbed
                    between fingers   ...Go to 6
   ioil will **not** polish   ...Go to 8

   ioil's **shape** can be changed   ...Go to 7
   ihape can **not** be changed   ...**Clay**

   The shape is easily changed   ...**Silty clay loam**

C

Ticks (✓) indicate the features shown by each soil type:

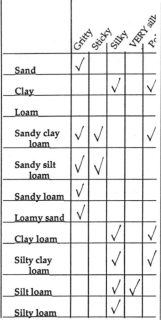

	Gritty	Sticky	Silky	VERY silky	P...
Sand	✓				
Clay			✓	✓	
Loam					
Sandy clay loam	✓	✓		✓	
Sandy silt loam	✓	✓			
Sandy loam	✓				
Loamy sand	✓				
Clay loam			✓	✓	
Silty clay loam			✓	✓	
Silt loam			✓	✓	
Silty loam			✓		

D

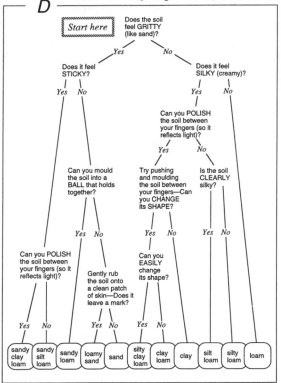

What about pictures?

Pictorial material—graphs, drawings, cartoons, photographs, maps, etc—can be used for many different purposes:

- **Decoration**   Simply to offer relief from the visual tedium of solid prose.

- **Amusement**   To touch on the lighter side of your subject (without trivializing, of course).

- **Expression**   To convey an emotion or stimulate feelings about the subject.

- **Persuasion**   To encourage learners towards a change of attitude or practice.

- **Illustration**   Superior form of decoration—where the picture enriches understanding of the text but is not strictly necessary to it.

- **Description**   To show what something looks like—in a way that words alone could not do.

- **Explanation**   To show not just what something looks like but also how it works or how to operate it.

- **Simplification**   To "edit" reality by cutting out aspects that would confuse or distract the user.

- **Quantification**   To represent different numbers and quantities with lines or areas of different size in graphs or charts.

- **Problem-posing**   To act as the focus of questions, encouraging analysis and investigation.

How many of these purposes can you find among the pictures on pages 114 and 120?

Some pictures from open learning materials

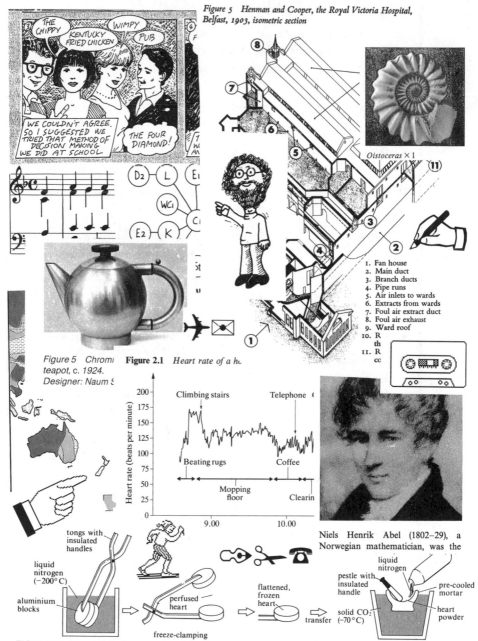

Figure 5   Henman and Cooper, the Royal Victoria Hospital, Belfast, 1903, isometric section

Oistoceras × 1

1. Fan house
2. Main duct
3. Branch ducts
4. Pipe runs
5. Air inlets to wards
6. Extracts from wards
7. Foul air extract duct
8. Foul air exhaust
9. Ward roof
10. R
    th
11. R
    co

Figure 5   Chromi teapot, c. 1924. Designer: Naum S

Figure 2.1   *Heart rate of a h*

Niels Henrik Abel (1802–29), a Norwegian mathematician, was the

FIGURE 3.1   Procedure for the preparation of extracts from organs or tissues. The tissue is rapidly frozen by clamping it between metal blocks precooled to nearly −200 °C. The frozen, flattened tissue is transferred to a mortar for pulverising and is kept frozen by direct addition of liquid nitrogen. The resulting powder is dispersed rapidly in ice-cold perchloric acid and the extract is finally neutralised with potassium hydroxide.

Development activities

1 If you'd like more ideas about graphic approaches, read:

   • TTSI (pages 181–206)

   • LOWE (1993).

              Then:

2 Think about how you might express some of your material more graphically than in solid prose— e.g. lists, tables, charts.

3 Select or produce some pictorial material for the package you are preparing. If possible, consult a graphic designer.

4 Show your ideas for graphics to colleagues and discuss how you plan to use them in your materials. If you can also discuss them with some learners, so much the better.

5 Revise your graphics as necessary in the light of the feedback you get. And consider how you might obtain more.

Checklist

• Have you considered all ways in which solid prose might be replaced by more graphic forms—e.g. lists or tables?

• Do you have any learning objectives for which pictures are essential?

• For which of the purposes mentioned on page 119 might you want to use pictures in your material?

• How much verbal explanation are learners likely to need if they are to get the most out of the pictures you are thinking of showing them?

• How certain are you that the pictures you have chosen will seem relevant and helpful to your learners?

• Can you see ways in which worthwhile activities might be based on pictures?

• Might you find it worthwhile to offer a series of still pictures (with captions) as a substitute for the moving pictures of a video?

• If you are producing an audio-cassette, are there any pictures that learners might usefully study while listening (audio-vision)?

• If you are using desktop publishing, have you explored dingbats, clip art, scanning in, paint-draw packages, and other means of producing computer graphics?

• Have you considered the use of old engravings and other out-of-copyright illustrations, many of which have been reprinted in source-books for designers?

• Do you have any friends or colleagues who may be able to take photographs for you, or draw cartoons or other pictures at reasonable cost?

• Can you think of other sources from which you might be able to get suitable graphic material?

> Keep a file of pictures you may want to use in the future—and a note of where to seek permission to reproduce them.

Task 2f

Decide on access devices

By the time you publish your materials, you will be very familiar with their structure. You'll know exactly how they hang together—how they are meant to work.

But learners won't have your familiarity. They'll face a pile of stuff and wonder how to get into it. How are they to find their way around in it? They could feel at a loss.

How might you guide your learners?

So what can you do to help them get to grips and find their way around? The chief thing you can do is provide them with what are sometimes called "access devices". These take many forms.

Are you chiefly concerned with printed material? If so, you may want to check through the main access devices I have listed overleaf.

If you are more concerned with other media, you may want to consider the suggestions in the display on page 126.

Using access devices in texts

*I have grouped these access devices according
to whether you would insert them near the beginning,
or during, or near the end of your materials
—or of a unit within them:*

Beginning
- Explanatory title
- Contents list
- Route map of package or unit
- Introduction/overview
- Links with other materials
- List of objectives
- Guidance on how to use the material
- Pre-test

During
- Headings
- Numbering systems
- Instructions about what to do next
- Verbal signposts (see page 125)
- Graphic signals (see page 125)
- Summaries

End
- Glossary
- Post-test
- Index

Any other access devices you might use?

*Of course, you can make the final decisions
about access devices at the editing stage.
But thinking about them early may help you
shape your first draft.*

Verbal signposts

*Phrases that let your learner know
where the argument is going—e.g.:*

"On the other hand . . . "

"Another example . . . "

"But that's not the only approach . . . "

"Now for something that may surprise you . . . "

"Let us turn aside for a moment to examine . . . "

"Now we come to the really tough part of the argument . . . "

"What this all adds up to is . . . "

Graphic signals—e.g.:

- **"White space"**. Open learning materials are often less densely printed than normal texts. Fewer words per page. Perhaps large boxes left for learners to write in.

- **"Reader-stoppers"**—e.g. rules of type across the page, meant to remind learners to pause and do an activity:

  ❖❖❖❖❖❖❖❖❖❖❖❖❖❖❖❖❖❖❖❖❖❖❖❖❖❖❖❖❖❖❖

- **Bulleted lists**. Like this one. Often better than solid text for showing that a number of points are related. "Bullets" (•) or other devices (~) make them stand out more clearly.

- **Tints and boxes.** Certain kinds of material—e.g. quotations or case studies—may regularly be boxed or tinted so that learners recognize it needs a special kind of attention.

- **Icons**. Graphic symbols used in the margin to tell learners what sort of material they are about to deal with. Those alongside, for example, might indicate (in order):

  ~ an activity

  ~ using a video

  ~ using audio material

  ~ referring to other printed material.

Access devices in other media

What access devices might your learners need if you are producing materials in media other than print? For instance:

- If your package consists of several media components, how are learners to know how they're all meant to fit together? (Labelling? Guide to contents? Flow diagram?)

- If you are producing a computer-based training package, how will you enable learners to find their way around in it and know where they've got to? (Menus? Screen headings? Route maps?)

- If you're producing audio or video cassettes, how might you help learners get as quickly as possible to a chosen point in the tape? (Marks on the label? Spoken "section numbers" on the audio? A clock showing elapsed time in the corner of the TV screen?)

- If you are providing a physical study area (e.g. an open learning centre), how are you to design that area so as to help learners know what is available and find what they need? (Labels? Posters? Colour codes? Catalogues? Help-line?)

o   *What else might you need to provide?*

Development activities

1 If you'd like more ideas about using access devices, read:

- TTSI (pages 163–79)

and look at some open learning materials to see how other writers have used them.

Then:

2 Write yourself a memo listing the access devices you plan to use in your materials and noting your ideas about what form they will take.

3 Discuss your ideas with a colleague.

4 Revise them if necessary.

Checklist

- The aim of access devices is to help learners find what is in your materials, get to the parts they need, and see how the parts relate to one another. Are you satisfied that your access devices will achieve that aim?

- Have you considered a possible role for each of the access devices listed on page 124?

- Have you thought of access devices you might use at the beginning and end of a complete package of materials (e.g. a course) as well as those you might use within each of the component units or sections?

- Have you been careful not to "over-egg the pudding" by having too many different access devices (especially graphic signals)?

- If you are using media other than print, have you still been able to think of appropriate access devices?

> By the way, you can't always assume that learners will know how to use all of your access devices. You may need to explain them.

Task 2g

Consider
the physical format

How will your materials look? How will they "handle"?
I ask this because it can affect your learners' learning.

If your materials look grotty, learners may ignore them. Or
pick them up with low expectations.

And if your materials are awkward to use or poorly packaged,
they may misuse them, abuse them, and lose bits of them.

How will it look?

It may be that you don't have any choice in such matters.
Maybe your materials are to fit into a series—and yours must
look much like everyone else's. Maybe someone else in your
organization decides about physical format.

All the same, it's important to have some idea about how the
package will look before you start writing. This may affect
how (and even what) you write.

Decisions to be made

And what if you **do** have some power to influence the
format? Well, there are several decisions to be made (see page
130). If you don't make them, someone else will—e.g. a word
processor operator, a printer, a technician. And they may not
know enough about the needs of your learners to make the
best ones. So let other people know your preferences as soon
as possible.

Physical format

Decisions are needed about:

- Packaging. (How are different components to be kept together—brown paper envelope, ring binder, custom-made box?)

- "Binding" of text—e.g. staples, glue, sewing, rings, comb, slide, etc.

- Paper quality—e.g. thickness and whiteness.

- Use of colour printing. (How many colours? Where?)

- Page size—A4, A5, etc.

- Pages to be used in "portrait" or "landscape" format —i.e. ☐ or ▭.

- Size of margins.

- Use of margins—e.g. for pictures, side-headings, icons.

- Number and shape of columns.

- Placing of illustrations—e.g. separate section, in margins, across columns, etc.

- Typeface(s)—fonts and point sizes. (See page 131.)

- Typestyle—plain, bold, italic, etc.

- Space between lines. (See page 132.)

- Length of lines. (See page 132.)

- Justified (straight) or ragged edges to blocks of type.

o *Others (What?)*

*If you don't make these decisions,
someone else will.*

Typefaces—character and point size

Some of the hundreds of typefaces available on laser printers.
Notice how they vary in "blackness" and in the amount of paper they cover.
The typeface in this paragraph is Helvetica Italic 10 point with 12 point
"leading" (the space between lines, pronounced "ledding").
The examples below are all 8 point, with 10 point leading.

Some of the hundreds of typefaces available on laser printers. Notice how they vary in "blackness" and in the amount of paper they cover. All of these examples are in 8 point, with 10 point "leading" (the space between lines). The typeface in this paragraph is PALATINO.

Some of the hundreds of typefaces available on laser printers. Notice how they vary in "blackness" and inthe amount of paper they cover. All of these examples are in 8 point, with 10point "leading" (the space between lines). The typeface in this paragraph is HELVETICA.

Some of the hundreds of typefaces available on laser printers. Notice how they vary in "blackness" and in the amount of paper they cover. All of these examples are in 8 point, with 10 point "leading" (the space between lines). The typeface in this paragraph is TIMES.

Some of the hundreds of typefaces available on laser printers. Notice how they vary in "blackness" and in the amount of paper they cover. All of these examples are in 8 point, with 12 point "leading" (the space between lines).The typeface in this paragraph is ARCHITECT.

Some of the hundreds of typefaces available on laser printers. Notice how they vary in "blackness" and in the amount of paper they cover. All of these examples are in 8 point, with 10 point "leading" (the space between lines). The typeface in this paragraph is GARAMOND NARROW.

Some of the hundreds of typefaces available on laser printers. Notice how they vary in "blackness" and in the amount of paper they cover. All of these examples are in 8 point, with 10 point "leading" (the space between lines). The typeface in this paragraph is NEW CENTURY SCHOOLBOOK.

Some of the hundreds of typefaces available on laser printers. Notice how they vary in "blackness" and in the amount of paper they cover. All of these examples are in 8 point, with 10 point "leading" (the space between lines). The typeface in this paragraph is SWING.

Some of the hundreds of typefaces available on laser printers. Notice how they vary in "blackness" and in the amount of paper they cover. All of these examples are in 8 point, with 10 point "leading" (the space between lines). The typeface in this paragraph is STONE.

> *All typefaces are available in many sizes, e.g.:*

12 point.

16 point.

24 point.

28 point.

36 point.

48 point.

Line length and spacing ("leading")

A common fault with open learning (and other) materials is to use too long a line of type. More often than not such materials are printed on A4 sheets, which are considerably wider than the traditional book page, and perhaps people feel they must avoid "wasting" paper by leaving wide margins. But long lines make for tiring reading. The reader's eyes, having swept to the end of one line, have trouble finding the start of the next line down. Unless you want your learner to suffer headaches—or else resort to the habit of reading with one finger keeping their place on the page—such long lines are best avoided. Fortunately, there are other ways of arranging print on an A4 page. Some of these are illustrated in the sample passages set out below.

One obvious way to ease your reader's task is to to use a shorter line (as here) and allow a wider margin. Usually, a line containing about 60–70 characters (allowing for the spaces as well as the letters) should give a length that can be read comfortably. But a longer line may be made readable if you increase the line spacing (as shown in the next sample). Increasing the type-size may have a similar effect.

If you want to take the full width of an A4 page, you may be able to use a line longer than 60–70 characters if you increase the spacing (as in this sample). Another alternative is to use two or more columns, perhaps with a smaller type-size (as in the final sample). The effect, however, unless you build in plenty of "white space", may be to produce pages so black with print that readers lose heart at the sight of them. Paper, remember, is always cheap compared with the cost of staff time that goes into developing materials. It is a pity to spoil the job by penny-pinching. White space and wide margins can have a role to play in helping your learners learn.

A common fault with open learning (and other) materials is to use too long a line of type. More often than not such materials are printed on A4 sheets, which are considerably wider than the traditional book page, and perhaps people feel they must avoid "wasting" paper by leaving wide margins. But long lines make for tiring reading. The reader's eyes, having swept to the end of one line, have trouble finding the start of the next line down. Unless you want your learner to suffer headaches—or else resort to the habit of reading with one finger keeping their place on the page—such long lines are best avoided. Fortunately, there are other ways of arranging print on an A4 page.

One way to ease your reader's task is to to use shorter lines (as in the second sample) and allow a wider margin. Usually, a line containing about 60–70 characters (allowing for the spaces as well as the letters) should give a length that can be read comfortably. But a longer line may be made readable if you increase the line spacing (as in the previous sample). Increasing the type-size may have a similar effect.

Another alternative is to use two or more columns, perhaps with a smaller type-size (as in this sample). The effect, however, unless you build in plenty of "white space", may be to produce pages so black with print that readers lose heart at the sight of them.

Paper, remember, is always cheap compared with the cost of staff time that goes into developing materials. It is a pity to spoil the job by penny-pinching. White space and wide margins can have a role to play in helping your learners learn.

Development activities

1 If you'd like more ideas about physical format, read:

- *TTSI (pages 275–299)*
- *MILES (1987)*
- *WHITE (1988)*

and look to see how other open learning materials have been put together.

Then:

2 Go through the list on page 130 of this book and decide which of the decisions you will be able to have some say in.

3 Discuss those decisions—and the grounds on which they might be made—with colleagues. You may find it useful to talk with a graphic designer and/or an editor.

4 Reach an understanding about format and bear this in mind while you write.

Checklist

- Are you satisfied that you've done all you can to get your materials packaged in a form as convenient as possible for your learners?

- If your package of materials is to contain more than one item, have you found ways of ensuring that items do not get detached and lost?

- Have you influenced as many as possible of the decisions mentioned on page 130?

- How favourably do you believe people will compare the design of your materials with that of the best materials you've seen produced by others?

- Have you a clear understanding of the layout and typography of your materials—which you can now use if preparing the materials yourself or in briefing a word processing operator or printer later on?

- The physical format chosen for your materials will be part of your organization's "image". Will it convey an appropriate message?

- And how do you think your materials will look and feel compared with the books, newspapers and magazines that your learners read for pleasure?

> *You may find it useful to start a reference collection of photocopied pages from other people's materials whose design you find admirable in one way or another.*

Stage 3

Writing and re-writing

Route map for materials preparation

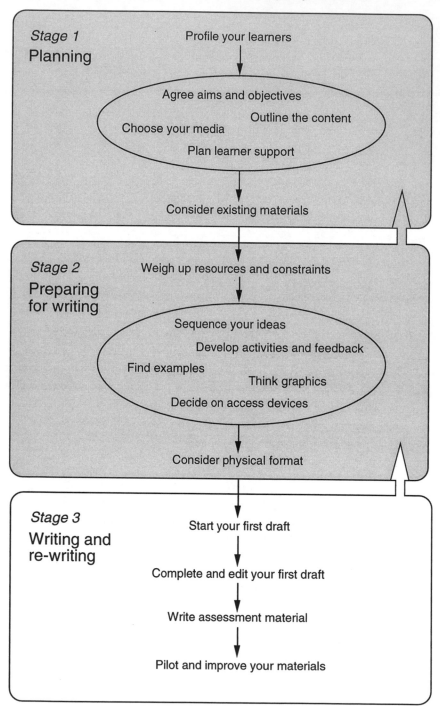

Stage 1
Planning

Profile your learners

Agree aims and objectives

Outline the content

Choose your media

Plan learner support

Consider existing materials

Stage 2
Preparing for writing

Weigh up resources and constraints

Sequence your ideas

Develop activities and feedback

Find examples

Think graphics

Decide on access devices

Consider physical format

Stage 3
Writing and re-writing

Start your first draft

Complete and edit your first draft

Write assessment material

Pilot and improve your materials

Task 3a
Start your first draft

Are you getting a bit nervous? All these tasks I've been setting you? All the time you may have put in? And perhaps not a single page of learning materials to show for it yet?

Well, don't worry. You'll find it was time well spent. It is not unusual for 50 per cent of the total project time to go on the two phases you have been through so far.

The wisest approach is to **think first and write afterwards**. There are two reasons for this:

- You'll probably write more fluently because you have a good overview of where you are going.
- You'll have already planned some pieces of the material (e.g. activities, examples, etc).

Getting started

So, let's begin. Four tips to get you going:

- Don't write more than three or four thousand words in Task 3a, before going on to Tasks 3b, 3c and 3d.
- Don't feel you must begin at the beginning. Maybe there's a bit in the middle you're especially looking forward to writing. If so, why not start there? Or maybe you'll be more confident once you've written the final summary?
- Write for **someone you know**. Bring to mind a couple of learners you've met—e.g. Bill and Sushma. Imagine you're talking to them—and keeping asking yourself how Sushma and Bill would react to what you're saying.
- Check through the displays on the following pages.

What must your writing bring about?

Your learning materials need to do for your learners just what a good teacher or coach would do if working with them face-to-face. For example:

• Get your learners interested.	*Help them see the benefits they'll get from the package—and from each section within it.*
• Remind them of any necessary prior learning.	*Check that learners have any prerequisite knowledge or skills.*
• Make clear what they will be learning next.	*Make sure they are in no doubt about the learning objectives.*
• Help them grasp the new ideas.	*By clear explanation, by helping them find out for themselves, or by a combination of the two.*
• Relate new ideas to learners' own experience.	*Get the learners to use their own examples and situations.*
• Get learners to think and do.	*Build in activities, projects, assignments that encourage them to work with the new ideas.*
• Help them get constructive feedback on what they do.	*Either from your materials or from other things and people.*
• Adapt the teaching to each individual's needs.	*By suggesting ways in which they can have contact with a tutor.*
• Enable them to reflect on their own progress.	*Provide tests that show how well they have attained the objectives.*
• Help them build on what they have learned.	*For instance, by using it in later sections of the material.*

~   *Activities and feedback will play a big part in accomplishing many of the above purposes.*

~   *So will your access devices, examples and graphics.*

~   *But what about your **style of writing**?*

How to be reader-friendly

Be conversational—plain-speaking—welcoming

To be conversational:

- Refer to yourself as "I" (or "we" if appropriate) and your learner as "you".

- Use contractions (you'll, that's, could've, etc) wherever it sounds natural.

- Why not use rhetorical questions (like this one)? They can help keep learners awake.

- Keep on your learners' wavelength—with references and analogies that touch on shared everyday experience.

- Exploit the "human angle" —by relating your subject to people wherever relevant.

To be welcoming:

- Say who you (and any co-authors) are and tell of your own experience of the subject.

- Remember that your learners may be of more than one sex, race, religion, age-range, level of physical ability, sexual orientation, and so on.

- Avoid language and examples that exclude or offend any of your learners.

To speak plainly:

- Cut out surplus words—e.g. not "at the present moment in time" but "now"; not "aggravation of the redundancy situation" but "more sackings".

- Use short (and usually more familiar) words—e.g. not "utilization" but "use"; not "dissemination of misinformation" but "spreading lies".

- Introduce specialist words ("jargon") with care.

- Prefer concrete to abstract words—e.g. not "mortalities were occasioned" but "people were killed".

- Prefer active rather than passive verb forms—e.g. not "changes were made" but "we made changes".

- Keep your sentences short—i.e. rarely more than 20 words —but vary their length.

- Keep their structure simple. (Watch those sub-clauses!)

- Keep paragraphs short (e.g. no fewer than three or four per page).

- Use helpful headings.

See page 140 for an illustration of the above points.

Making it reader-friendly

An example from course materials

"The term ideology is used in this module to indicate a system of interpretation or belief held by a particular group or class (a political party, profession or voluntary organization, for example). The frameworks of understanding and interpretation contained within an ideological position are likely to represent and express the material and cultural interests of the particular group in question, and it is this factor which gives the concept of ideology its political dimension. Although a system of beliefs requires some degree of coherence to qualify as an ideology, elements of internal contradiction may also be expected as individuals have to continually reassess and recreate the terms of their understanding of events. Some ideologies therefore can be defined precisely, but some are more diffuse, and it is common for ideological differences to exist between individuals who are apparently members of the same group."

A possibly more reader-friendly version

As you've just seen in those two examples, different groups of people have different ways of looking at the world. This brings us to a term we'll be using often in this module—**ideology**.

What do we mean by ideology? The term refers to the set of beliefs that are common among a given group of people. Different political parties have their different ideologies. So do different professions. So do people in different organizations. They all see the world differently.

You'll usually find that a group's ideology tells you about what it wants for itself and how it plans to get or keep whatever power it has. This is why ideology is a political concept.

We don't normally say a group's set of beliefs is an ideology unless people in that group agree about most of them. However, this is not to say that all members of a group will agree in every detail. Individuals are always likely to be rethinking their positions on this aspect or that. So, although we can define some ideologies precisely, others may contain a range of views. That is, people in a group may agree on most issues but, on some, individuals may show what we call "ideological differences". Let's look at some further examples.

This is only one of many possible "translations".
Is it what the author meant? How might it be improved still further?

One way of measuring your readability

Fog Index

1 Calculate the average number of words per sentence in a passage.

2 Add on the percentage of words with three or more syllables.

3 Multiply by 0.4. (i.e. multiply by 4 and divide by 10.)

If the result—the Fog Index—is **more than 12**, your text could be too difficult for most of your readers. (See GUNNING, 1968.)

Our example from page 140—with "long words" in bold:

The term *ideology* is used in this module to **indicate** a system of **interpretation** or belief held by a **particular** group or class (a **political** party, **profession** or **voluntary organization**, for **example**). The frameworks of **understanding** and **interpretation** contained within an **ideological position** are likely to **represent** and express the **material** and **cultural interests** of the **particular** group in question, and it is this factor which gives the concept of **ideology** its **political dimension**. Although a system of beliefs requires some degree of **coherence** to **qualify** as an **ideology**, **elements** of **internal contradiction** may also be **expected** as **individuals** have to **continually reassess** and **recreate** the terms of their **understanding** of events.

No. of sentences = 3

No. of words = 112

Average no. of words per sentence = 37

No. of 3 (or more)-syllable words = 33

% of words with 3 (or more) syllables = 33 x 100/112 = 29

Fog Index = (37 + 29) x 0.4 = 26

You may like to calculate the Fog Index for our **revised** version of this passage. (I make it just under 12—much more acceptable, but still not an easy read.)

NOTE: If you are using a word processor,
you may be able to get a package that will do this
calculation for you.

If you can't get started . . .

*If you still can't get started—or, having started,
get bogged down—try this approach:*

- Take each of your sub-objectives in turn.

- Write one or more activities that will lead up to
  or provide practice with each sub-objective.

- Write whatever text is needed to get your learner
  from one activity to the next.

*Quite a few writers have found that this
seemingly back-to-front approach has
been just what they needed to
get themselves unblocked.*

Development activities

1 If you'd like more ideas about writing style, read:

- *TTSI (pages 207–232)*
- *GOWERS (1980)*
- *GUNNING (1968).*

2 Make sure you have in front of you the materials you've drafted during previous tasks—e.g. implications list, objectives, teaching points.

3 Write the first three or four thousand words of your material.

4 Review the reader-friendliness of your material so far, using the following checklist. (You may want to get a colleague to look at your work also—but I suggest you leave that until the next Task.)

5 Make any necessary changes to your material so far. Then:

6 Go on to Task 3b.

NOTE: You may find it worth checking the style and readability of some of the publications your learners read for pleasure. How will yours compare?

Checklist

- Is it easy to pick out the teaching point in each paragraph?

- Have you avoided complex sentences—those that sprout a tangle of clauses and phrases?

- Are your sentences reasonably short (but varied) in length?

- Can you see any passive verb forms that you want to make active?

- Can you see any vague, abstract words that you might want to make more concrete and precise?

- Can you see any long words (probably of Greek or Roman origin) that you might replace with shorter (probably Anglo-Saxon) ones?

- Have you used any specialist terms or acronyms without explaining them?

- Have you managed to avoid gobbledygook—vague, long-winded, mind-boggling phrases?

- Have you allowed your personality (if only your professional personality) to come through?

- Will your learners feel that a real person (rather than a committee or a computer) is addressing them?

- Are your examples welcoming to the diversity of people you are likely to have among your learners?

- Have you been careful to avoid language and examples that are sexist, racist, ageist, etc?

- Is your Fog Index always below 12?

- What have you learned from Task 3a that will help you as you carry on to complete your draft?

> *Always read your work ALOUD.*
> *If it sounds pompous, obscure or*
> *long-winded, it probably is.*

Task 3b

Complete and edit your first draft

So you've written and reflected on your first few thousand words. Now you are probably keen to get on and complete the first draft of your materials. Even so, if you're thinking of writing more than three or four hours' worth of learning material, I'd suggest you go through Tasks 3c and 3d each time you have produced about that much. That will give you more chance to learn from feedback as you go along.

Five things to do

There are five main things to do within this Task:

- Get a batch of materials written. (Make a note of any changes you make to your earlier ideas about objectives, content, assessment, etc.)

- Edit them into a form fit to be seen by other people. You may need to review the decisions you made in Tasks 2e, 2f and 2g. (See the checklist on page 146.)

- Collect comments on your material from colleagues who are prepared to act as "critical friends"—and from clients, if you have any. Discuss your timetable with them as soon as possible. They'll need to know how much time you'll be expecting from them, and when. (See the sample checklists on page 147.)

- Keep a cool head about the comments you get. Don't despair or over-react if colleagues suggest lots of changes. Don't get complacent if they don't. Sit back and think about your learners. What changes might benefit them?

- Revise your materials ready for piloting with learners in Task 3d. (And don't forget about getting copyright permissions. See page 148.)

An author's checklist

*Some of the questions you might ask
about your drafts:*

Objectives

- Have I stated the objectives—for the whole, for each part?
- Do they seem relevant to what we know of learners' needs?
- Are they stated in terms that readers will understand?

Activities

- Are there appropriate activities relating to the objectives?
- Are learners likely to think them worth doing?
- Have I given appropriate feedback (or suggested how learners might obtain their own)?

Subject content

- Are my explanations sufficiently clear and complete?
- Have I properly introduced new terms and concepts?
- Are examples plentiful and appropriate?
- Is any of the material redundant?
- Does it hang together logically?

Teaching structure

- Is the material split up into manageable chunks?
- Are its sub-sections marked out clearly with headings?
- Have I given introductions and summaries where appropriate?
- Is study guidance given where appropriate?
- Are lists used where preferable to solid text?
- Are diagrams, tables and graphics used where needed?
- Have I brought in other media where preferable?

Presentation

- Is my writing reader-friendly ("you" and "I" or "we")?
- Is it plain and simple (short words and short sentences)?
- Does the author seem to be on the learners' wavelength?
- Have I tried to bring the learners' experience into play?

Design

- Is the material attractive to look at and handle?
- Is the design appropriate to how the material will be used?

*NOTE: You may want to draw up your own checklist,
using this one as a basis.*

Sample checklists for critical commenting

Ask **subject experts** about *content and treatment*

- Are the aims and objectives sufficiently explicit?

- Do they seem worthwhile and relevant?

- Are there any further aims and objectives that should be tackled?

- Is the content appropriate to the objectives?

- Is it factually correct?

- Is it up-to-date?

- Any redundant material or important omissions ?

- Does the material hang together logically?

- Does it avoid over-simplification and over-generalization?

- Are all key statements supported by evidence?

- Does it contain any unsatisfactory examples, analogies, or case studies?

- *Other points?*

Ask **tutors** about *likely teaching effectiveness*

- Will learners (and tutors or mentors?) understand what is expected of them?

- Do you foresee learners having difficulty with any of the objectives?

- Is it pitched at the right level of difficulty and challenge?

- Do the examples, analogies and case studies seem relevant to learners' interests and are they sufficiently illuminating?

- Can you identify any sections likely to give learners problems? Why?

- Are all new terms/concepts adequately explained?

- Are all the activities and/or self-tests worthwhile, relevant to objectives and practicable?

- Do the assignments or suggested follow-up activities seem appropriate?

- Can you suggest any additional examples, activities, etc?

- *Other points?*

What questions do you need to ask YOUR "commenters"?

Copyright—ignore it at your peril!

- Anything one writes or creates—shopping lists, memos to the boss, textbooks, novels, photographs, maps, television programmes, films, music scores or recordings, computer programs, etc, etc—is automatically protected by the international copyright conventions.

- The protection lasts at least 50 years.

- Only the owner of the copyright (usually the creator) can grant you permission to copy from the material.

- If you copy without permission, you may be prosecuted.

- Permission may not be needed for a small extract (up to 400 words) from a lengthy work. But, to be safe, I would suggest you seek permission for an extract as small as 50 words—and you **must** if it exceeds 10% of the whole work (as in a poem or newspaper article).

- Write to the copyright owner (usually c/o a publisher), saying:

  ~ exactly what parts of their material you want to use—e.g. give page numbers or send a photocopy or a tape

  ~ any deletions or changes you might want to make

  ~ the context in which you plan to publish it—form, number of copies, internal use or generally available, free or priced, etc

  ~ whether you are hoping they will waive any fee (if the extract is small, or your project a "worthy" one) or whether you are willing to pay

  ~ that you will acknowledge the source.

- Make it as easy as possible for them—e.g. by sending a stamped envelope and a standard letter confirming permission which they may simply sign.

- For detailed guidance, consult: *Copyright Clearance: a practical guide* (3rd edition) by Geoffrey Crabb, National Council for Educational Technology, London, 1990.

*NOTE: If you can't get permission, don't despair. Only the published form is copyright, not the ideas behind it. You may still be able to express such ideas in a **new** form of your own.*

Development activities

1 If you'd like more ideas about critical commenting, read:

- *TTSI* (pages 333–8)

If you want more ideas about editing, read:

- *TTSI* (pages 363–77)—but for guidance on copyright, see:

- *CRABB (1990)*.

2 Find some colleagues willing and ready to act as 'critical friends'. Let them know when you expect to have some material for them to comment on. (You may also have clients who will need to comment.)

3 Write two or three hours' worth of material.

4 Critique and improve it yourself as you did in Task 3a.

5 Prepare checklists for your commenters, perhaps using those on page 147 as a basis.

6 Get written comments from your colleagues (and clients, if any). Discuss these with them if it seems useful.

7 Make any alterations to your materials that seem essential before trying them out with learners in Task 3d.

Checklist

- Have you kept up the level of reader-friendliness you set for yourself in Task 3a?

- Have you given information about the names and backgrounds of the authors—(photographs even)?

- Are learners given proper guidance about what they are supposed to be doing—at the start, during, and at the end of each sequence?

- How do you feel your materials measure up against the checklist on page 146? How might you improve them?

- Have you agreed everything you need to agree with any production colleagues—e.g. word processing operators, technicians, designers, editors—who will be helping you bring out your materials?

- Have you made best possible use of their professional advice—bowing to it where appropriate but not losing sight of your learners' needs?

- Have you sent off for any necessary copyright permission?

- Without seeking 100 per cent perfection (which no one has ever achieved), are you satisfied that your material looks as well as it might and reads as well as it should before you put it in the hands of your "critical friends"?

- Did you get enough feedback on all the aspects of your materials that you wanted comments about? If not, how might you get more?

- Did the commenting show up additional aspects that may need your attention? If so, can the commenters give you useful suggestions?

- If you've had comments from clients, can you see how to satisfy them?

- Have you made all alterations that will be necessary before your learners see the materials in Task 3d?

- What have you learned in this Task that will help you with the **next** batch of learning material you prepare?

Q. What's the secret of writing quality materials? A. Re-writing.

Task 3c
Write assessment material

Assessment enables you (or colleagues) to find out how learners have coped with your materials. There may be several reasons why assessment might be called for, e.g.:

- To provide a spur and a focus for learners' efforts.

- To pace them with regular tests or assignments.

- To enable individual help to be given to learners (e.g. on the basis of how they perform on assignments).

- To report on their achievements to sponsors and other interested parties (including themselves).

- To award credits, certificates, VQs, etc.

You may have yet other reasons for assessing. And you may already have started thinking about how best to do it. Writing detailed objectives often leads one to wonder "How would I get the learner to **demonstrate** this?"

Anyway, now is probably the time to firm up your ideas about assessment. But just what assessment materials might you need to produce?

See the next page for my suggestions.

What you'll need

Before you can sensibly pilot your learning materials with learners in Task 3d, you may well want to produce at least two kinds of assessment materials:

* A set of test questions or instructions for a workplace practical test or written assignments—or whatever is needed to prompt learners to show how well they have attained the objectives. (Often called post-tests.)

* Guidance notes, rating scales, performance checklists—or whatever will be needed by the people (tutors, managers, you?) who will be carrying out the assessment.

You may also need to produce:

* Guidance for the learners—e.g. notes explaining how the assessment scheme works, advice on how to prepare themselves, specimen test papers and specimen answers.

* Materials to assess learners' understanding or competence **before they begin** on your learning materials. (Pre-tests.)

Product v performance assessment

Which kind to use when?

1 Product assessment—*e.g. assessment of essays, worked calculations, multiple-choice tests, project reports, drawings, constructions—where there is a physical* **product** *to assess.*

A *"Own answer" tests*—

where the learner:

- writes, e.g.:
  - ~ a word or phrase or number
  - ~ a paragraph or short memo
  - ~ an essay or report
  - ~ an extended project report

- or makes something, e.g.:
  - ~ a drawing or photograph
  - ~ a computer program
  - ~ a 3-D object (e.g. a cake, a floral display, or a model bridge)

- **"Own-answer"** tests are needed if your objectives require learners to be able to recall, define, explain, justify, report, invent, sketch out, argue a case, or otherwise **produce something of their own**.

  NOTE: *Multiple-choice questions would not enable you to make an accurate assessment of those abilities.*

B *"Objective tests"*—

usually composed of multiple-choice questions—e.g.:

- ~ "one from several"
- ~ "two or more from several"
- ~ "true-false"
- ~ "matching"
- ~ "ranking"

- **Objective tests**—for when your objectives will be properly satisfied by having the learner **choose** from among a given set of possible answers —e.g. alternative terms, ideas, definitions, quantities, sounds, smells, pictures, actions, objects, or whatever is relevant.

2 Performance assessment—*i.e. assessment of an activity or* **process** *that may or may not result in any physical product.*

Might involve:

- demonstration of workplace competence
- a simulation of workplace performance
- demonstration of practical or social skills
- interviews
- oral testing (*viva voce*)

- **Performance assessment** is needed if your objectives are concerned with **how** your learners do or make something, or **how** they interact with other people.

  NOTE: *Product assessment would not be an accurate substitute for watching them, or listening to them do it.*

Make sure your assessment really tests what you want it to test—rather than something related but different.

Towards an assessment strategy . . .

*Some of the questions you may need to answer if you are planning an assessment strategy for a lengthy course. They may also help you plan how your **pilot** learners should be assessed.*

- For what **purposes** are we assessing—e.g. to help the learner improve his or her learning or to report on that learning to someone else?

- **What** shall we assess—e.g. which areas of knowledge, understanding, attitudes, practical competence?

- **When** shall we assess—e.g. at intervals during the course and/or at the end of it?

- **How much time** is it reasonable to expect learners to spend on the assessment exercises?

- **How** shall we assess—e.g. using what mix of product and performance approaches?

- **Who** will develop the assessment materials?

- Will those people need **training**?

- **Who** will do the assessing?

- What **help** might those assessors need—e.g. guidance materials, briefing and training, monitoring?

- **Who** will provide such help?

- **How** can learners be provided with appropriate feedback that will further their learning?

- If any of the assessment is to be done at a distance—by assessors who have not met the learners—what **special problems** might arise?

- What **standards of quality** might clients and customers (e.g. learners and their sponsors) expect in the assessment of learners?

You will no doubt be able to think of yet other questions that need answering in your own system.

Development activities

1 If you'd like more ideas about writing assessment material for learners and assessors, read:

   • TTSI (pages 301–32); and, if you're interested in a wider perspective on assessment, read:

   • ROWNTREE (1987).

2 Draft tests and assignments or whatever will be needed to find out how well your learners have attained their objectives.

3 Draft some guidance notes, rating scales, performance checklists or whatever will be needed by people who will be asked to appraise and comment on your learners' work.

4 Arrange for some critical commenting from colleagues— preferably from those who will be responsible for carrying out the assessment. (Consult some learners also, if you can.)

5 Discuss the comments you've received with your colleagues.

5 Improve your assessment materials in the light of the feedback.

Checklist

• Have you found a way of testing all your important objectives?

• Are you sure that none of your assessment exercises are really testing some other (perhaps more easily testable) objectives instead?

• If your materials are aimed at improving your learners' workplace competence, have you found a way of testing their competence in a real or simulated workplace?

• Have you given your learners sufficiently clear and unambiguous guidance so they will know exactly what you are expecting them to do?

• If you are planning a final exam as well as occasional tests or assignments (course work), what special purpose is it meant to serve?

• Have you provided all necessary guidance for assessors— e.g. correct answers, specimen answers, marking schemes, performance checklists?

• If you've provided correct answers (e.g. for objective tests), are you absolutely sure they **are** all correct?

• Is your guidance for assessors so clear and unambiguous that you can be sure all will be looking for the same competences and responding to them in the same way?

• Are your assessment activities likely to take up a reasonable amount of the learners' time—compared with the time they'll have spent on the learning materials?

• Have you thought how the assessment might help in adapting the teaching to individual learners' needs?

• Have you thought of ways of ensuring that learners get feedback as to how they have done on the assessment?

> *Try to make assessment part of the learning experience—not something that happens only when it's all over.*

Task 3d

Pilot and improve your materials

This could be the most crucial task in the whole project. You've drafted some materials that you and your colleagues are pretty happy with. Fine. But what about the learners? Until your material's been tried out by the people you wrote it for, you still can't be sure how closely it will suit their needs. Or decide how it must be improved.

So all three steps are vital in producing quality material:

Write it—Try it out—Improve it.

Getting feedback about the acceptability and effectiveness of our materials is usually called "evaluation". Evaluation takes three main forms:

- **Critical commenting**—which I suggested as part of Tasks 3b and 3c.

- **Piloting**—sometimes called developmental testing. (We concentrate on this during the present task.)

- **Continuous monitoring**—collecting feedback throughout the life of the materials. (You may need to give some thought to how this might be done.)

Who wants to know?

You may not be the only one who wants to know how your materials work in practice. Which of the following might also be interested in the results of your piloting?

• Your co-authors (if any)	Especially those writing materials that lead up to yours or carry on where yours leave off.
• Other colleagues e.g. managers	For instance, they may be concerned with quality criteria, costing, scheduling, public relations, and so on.
• Committees, etc	Influential groups of people whom you want to inform and/or who feel they should know.
• Accrediting bodies	Do your materials satisfy the bodies' criteria?
• Your clients	Anyone who is funding the project and looking for some kind of return.
• Learners' sponsors or line managers	People wondering about the suitability of your materials for their staff.
• Consultants	Experts whose advice you have sought while developing the materials.
• Marketing agencies	People who will be promoting your materials to potential learners.
• Pilot learners and tutors	Who may be interested to hear how their response to the materials compares with those of others who assisted you.
• Future learners/users	How might your pilot guide them?
• *Others? (Who?)*	What might be their interest?

How will you cater for the concerns of such "interested parties" in designing your piloting? How will you report to them the results they might find helpful?

Two forms of piloting

Face-to-face tryouts

- Find two or three learners who are typical of those you are writing for.

- Ask them to help you find any weaknesses or difficulties in the material.

- Sit with them, one at a time, while they work through it.

- Make a note of any problems they seem to be having.

- Talk it over with them afterwards, and get their suggestions.

- If they point out things that you think may trouble other learners also, change them.

Field trials

- Get the agreement of a number of learners (preferably 20–30 but half a dozen is better than nothing) to work though your materials in as near as possible "normal conditions".

- This may mean you'll need to provide them with a tutor, a help-line, meetings with other learners, back-up from their line manager, or whatever other kind of support you decided your materials would need.

- Prepare any log-sheets you want your learners to fill in during their work, or questionnaires you want them to complete afterwards.

- Get them to work through the materials (including any assignments or tests).

- Collect the log-sheets, questionnaires, test results, etc and decide what they suggest about your materials in use.

- Discuss the results with a group of your pilot learners if possible (and with their supporters, if any).

- Improve the package before publishing it for general use.

Issues you may want to enquire about in questionnaires or discussions

Theoretical instruction
- Clarity of course aims and objectives.
- Relevance of content to aims and objectives.
- Adaptability of content/objectives to learners' interests.
- Adequacy of study time suggested/allowed.
- Suitability of teaching methods and media.
- Availability of personal guidance.

Practical work
- Coverage of all necessary skills.
- Relation of theory to practice.
- Adequacy of preparation for practical work.
- Availability of feedback/personal guidance on practical skills.
- Relation of practical exercises to "real-life" situations.

Assessment
- Appropriateness of the assessments.
- Clarity of information given about assessment.
- Helpfulness of feedback to the learners.
- Availability of individual help where difficulties occur.

General evaluation of course (so far)
- Responsiveness of system to learners' needs.
- Each learner's perceptions of what he or she has gained.
- Most/least satisfactory features of the course.
- Suggestions for improvements from learners.

You may want to raise these issues—with supporters as well as with learners—during continuous monitoring as well as during piloting.

Development activities

1 If you'd like more ideas about evaluating materials, read:

   • TTSI (pages 338–60) and, for a wider perspective on evaluation,

   • EXPLODL (pages 203–29)

2 Do a face-to-face tryout with two or three learners.

3 If they raise problems that you think future learners may have also, amend your materials where necessary.

4 Run a field trial—getting some typical learners to work through your material (including the assessment) under the kind of conditions it will normally be used in. (You may need to provide some human support, if that would be part of those 'normal conditions'.)

5 Analyse the feedback you get, with the help of colleagues and the checklist overleaf.

6 Improve your materials.

7 Go on to write more.

Checklist

- On the basis of the assessment results, how happy are you about what your learners have learned?

- If your materials were meant to improve learners' workplace competence, did they?

- What have you learned about the ways in which learners used the materials?

- What has the piloting told you about how long your learners are likely to take over the materials? Will this amount of time seem realistic for them? If not, what can be cut out?

- Were there any problems (or opportunities) that you didn't expect?

- How successful was the material you provided for support staff—e.g. tutors, assessors? Does it need improving?

- What changes do you need to make in your materials (or in the support system) before they go into regular use?

- Do you need to write a report on the piloting—e.g. for your boss, or for clients, or for the learners?

- If you have clients, how happy are they with the results?

- How might you use what you have learned from the pilot in recruiting future learners or in marketing the materials to potential sponsors?

- Has the piloting given you any ideas about what might be done during "continuous monitoring"—to collect feedback about the use of the materials in the future?

- What have you learned from the piloting that will help you in writing your next batch of materials?

Well, I hope that was enough to get you started. I wish you every success in developing your future materials—and your learners every success in using them.

Further reading

Crabb, G. (1990) *Copyright Clearance: a practical guide* (3rd edn),
National Council for Educational Technology, London

DCfS—Rowntree, D. (1985) *Developing Courses for Students*,
Paul Chapman, London

EXPLÓDL—Rowntree, D. (1992) *Exploring Open and Distance
Learning*, Kogan Page, London

Gowers, E. (1980) *The Complete Plain Words* (2nd edn),
Penguin, Harmondsworth

Gunning, R. (1968) *The Technique of Clear Writing*, McGraw-
Hill, New York

Kember, D. (1991) *Writing Study Guides*, Technical and
Educational Services, Bristol

Laurillard, D. (1993) *Rethinking University Teaching: a
Framework for the Effective Use of Educational Technology*,
Routledge, London

Lewis, R. & Paine, N. (1986) *How to Find and Adapt Materials
and Select Media*, Council for Educational Technology,
London

Lockwood, F. (1992) *Activities in Self-instructional Texts*, Kogan
Page, London

Lowe, R. (1993) *Successful Instructional Diagrams*, Kogan Page,
London

Mager, R. (1990) *Preparing Instructional Objectives* (2nd edn),
Kogan Page, London

Miles, J. (1987) *Design for Desktop Publishing*, John Taylor Book
Ventures, Hatfield, Herts

Morgan, A. (1993) *Improving your Students' Learning*, Kogan
Page, London

Rowntree, D. (1985) *Developing Courses for Students*, Paul
Chapman, London

Rowntree, D. (1987) *Assessing Students: How Shall we Know
Them?*, Kogan Page, London

Rowntree, D. (1990) *Teaching Through Self-instruction*, Kogan
Page, London

Rowntree, D. (1992) *Exploring Open and Distance Learning*, Kogan Page, London

Rowntree, D. (1994) *Teaching with Audio in Open and Distance Learning*, Kogan Page, London

Thorpe, M. (1993) *Evaluating Open and Distance Learning* (2nd edn), Longmans, Harlow

TTSI—Rowntree, D. (1990) *Teaching Through Self-instruction*, Kogan Page, London

White, J.V. (1988) *Graphic Design for the Electronic Age*, Watson-Guptill Publications, New York

If you need further support . . .

I hope this book has been of help to you. If you or your colleagues need any more direct help, you may like to know that I run regular **workshops** for

a) people who are just about to begin writing open learning materials—and are perhaps looking for a kindly kick-start! and

b) people who have already written their first batch of material and want to bring it along to discuss it with me and other writers.

In addition, I am often asked to write a **constructive critique** of an author's learning material—offering my suggestions for developing or improving it—a kind of consultancy at a distance.

If you are interested in any of these services, please contact me c/o my publishers:

> Kogan Page Ltd
> 120 Pentonville Road
> London N1 9JN

Index

Other books on open learning
by Derek Rowntree

Teaching Through Self-instruction
—how to develop open learning materials

There is no one right way to produce quality open learning materials
. . . but there are plenty of wrong ways.
This book should help you avoid them.

"If you were only to buy one book on open learning materials you could hardly do better than this one."
Hilary Temple in *TRANSITION*

Publisher:
Kogan Page Ltd, 120 Pentonville Rd, London N1 9JN

Exploring Open and Distance Learning

A book that puts the development of materials into a wider perspective

Unit 1   What are open and distance learning?
Unit 2   Open learners and their learning
Unit 3   Supporting open learners
Unit 4   Media in open learning
Unit 5   The package in open learning
          Sample pages from open learning materials
Unit 6   What does open learning cost?
Unit 7   Evaluating open learning
Unit 8   The pros and cons of open learning
Unit 9   Implementing open learning

Publisher:
Kogan Page Ltd, 120 Pentonville Rd, London N1 9JN

Teach Yourself with Open Learning

The book your learners need to prepare them for open learning

Chapter 1   Welcome to open learning
Chapter 2   You and your learning
Chapter 3   What can open learning offer you?
Chapter 4   How does open learning work?
Chapter 5   Choosing your open learning programme
Chapter 6   Getting organized for open learning
Chapter 7   How to tackle your package
Chapter 8   How to get help from other people
Chapter 9   Are you getting value for money?

Publisher:
Kogan Page Ltd, 120 Pentonville Rd, London N1 9JN